Your Negativity Fingerprint

Practical Strategies to Overcome Negative Thinking, Stress, and Anxiety

Lorena E. Hammond

© Copyright 2024 - All rights reserved.

The content contained within this book may not be reproduced, duplicated or transmitted without direct written permission from the author or the publisher.

Under no circumstances will any blame or legal responsibility be held against the publisher, or author, for any damages, reparation, or monetary loss due to the information contained within this book, either directly or indirectly.

Legal Notice:

This book is copyright protected. It is only for personal use. You cannot amend, distribute, sell, use, quote or paraphrase any part, or the content within this book, without the consent of the author or publisher.

Disclaimer Notice:

Please note the information contained within this document is for educational and entertainment purposes only. All effort has been executed to present accurate, up to date, reliable, complete information. No warranties of any kind are declared or implied. Readers acknowledge that the author is not engaged in the rendering of legal, financial, medical or professional advice. The content within this book has been derived from various sources. Please consult a licensed professional before attempting any techniques outlined in this book.

By reading this document, the reader agrees that under no circumstances is the author responsible for any losses, direct or indirect, that are incurred as a result of the use of the information contained within this document, including, but not limited to, errors, omissions, or inaccuracies.

Table of Contents

INTRODUCTION: THE PERVASIVE PROBLEM OF NEGATIVE THINKING 1

PART 1: UNDERSTANDING NEGATIVE THINKING 5

CHAPTER 1: THE SCIENCE BEHIND NEGATIVE THOUGHTS 7

What Is Negative Thinking? 7
Biological Factors: It's Not Just All in Your Head (Well, It Is, but You Know What I Mean) 9
Psychological Factors: Your Brain's Favorite Tricks 9
Neuroplasticity: Your Brain's Superpower (and Sometimes Its Kryptonite) . 10
Key Takeaways and What's Next 11

CHAPTER 2: THE VICIOUS CYCLE— HOW NEGATIVE THOUGHTS FEED ANXIETY AND STRESS 13

The Relationship Between Negative Thoughts, Anxiety, and Stress 13
The Snowball Effect: How It All Spirals Out of Control 14
The Cycle Breakdown: Your Emergency Exit Strategy 15
Key Takeaways and What's Next 16

CHAPTER 3: POSITIVE PSYCHOLOGY— THE ANTIDOTE TO NEGATIVITY? 19

What Is Positive Psychology? 19
The Importance of Positive Psychology 20
How to Apply Positive Psychology Principles 21
Case Studies Relating to Positive Psychology 22
Scientific Research to Support Positive Psychology 22
Key Takeaways and What's Next 23

CHAPTER 4: THE HIDDEN COSTS OF CHRONIC NEGATIVE THINKING 25

The Physical Costs of Chronic Negative Thinking 26
The Mental Health Impact 27
Relationship Strains and Professional Setbacks Due to Negative Thinking . 27
How Negative Thinking Can Limit Personal Growth and Happiness 28
Key Takeaways and What's Next 29

.... 30

PART 2: IDENTIFYING YOUR NEGATIVE THOUGHT PATTERNS 31

CHAPTER 5: THE 7 MOST COMMON NEGATIVE THINKING TRAPS AND DISCOVERING YOUR UNIQUE "NEGATIVITY FINGERPRINT" 33

The 7 Most Common Negative Thinking Traps................................33
How to Identify Which Trap(s) You Frequently Fall Into 35
Your Unique "Negativity Fingerprint"...36
Practical Strategies to Overcome Each Trap 37
Key Takeaways and What's Next 39

CHAPTER 6: NEGATIVE SELF-TALK AND THE STORIES WE TELL OURSELVES 41

What Is Negative Self-Talk?..41
Types of Negative Self-Talk 42
The Stories We Tell Ourselves 43
Changing Our Narratives 44
Key Takeaways and What's Next 45

CHAPTER 7: ABSORBING NEGATIVITY FROM OTHERS 47

What Is Emotional Contagion? The Science of Catching Feelings 47
Identifying Sources of External Negativity...................................48
Protecting Yourself From Absorbing Negativity 49
Managing Relationships With Negative Individuals......................51
Key Takeaways and What's Next 52

PART 3: PROVEN STRATEGIES TO BREAK FREE OF NEGATIVITY 55

CHAPTER 8: THE "THOUGHT REPLACEMENT" TECHNIQUE FOR CONQUERING NEGATIVE THOUGHTS 57

Understanding Thought Replacement...57
The Science Behind Thought Replacement 58
Implementing Thought Replacement 58
When the Going Gets Tough: Challenges and Solutions.................59
Key Takeaways and What's Next 61

CHAPTER 9: HARNESSING THE IMPORTANCE OF GRATITUDE...................... 63

The Science Behind Gratitude..63
Benefits of Practicing Gratitude 64
How to Cultivate Gratitude..65
Key Takeaways and What's Next 67

CHAPTER 10: MINDFULNESS, AFFIRMATIONS, AND MANTRAS TO REWIRE YOUR BRAIN 69

Understanding Mindfulness, Affirmations, and Mantras...............69
The Science Behind Rewiring Your Brain 70
Practical Steps to Incorporate These Techniques 71

Key Takeaways and What's Next.. *73*

CHAPTER 11: CHALLENGING NEGATIVE THOUGHTS WITH REASON AND EVIDENCE **75**

Cognitive Distortions *75*
The Role of Evidence in Challenging Negative Thoughts *79*
Techniques for Gathering Evidence Against Negative Thoughts *81*
Case Studies *82*
Key Takeaways and What's Next *83*

CHAPTER 12: TURNING NEGATIVES INTO POSITIVES—THE ART OF REFRAMING, VISUALIZATION AND THE "YES, BUT" TRICK **85**

Understanding Reframing *85*
Steps for Reframing Negative Thoughts *86*
What Is Visualization and How Can It Help Reframe Thoughts? *87*
Types of Visualization Exercises for Positive Thinking and How to Use It *88*
Understanding the "Yes, But" Technique *89*
Key Takeaways and What's Next *90*

CHAPTER 13: OVERCOMING NEGATIVITY IN KEY LIFE AREAS **93**

Silencing Your Inner Critic at Work and Dealing With Others *93*
Impact of Negative Thinking on Relationships *98*
Conquering Negative Thinking about Your Body, Appearance and Aging *103*
Releasing Negativity Surrounding Money and Finances *107*
Key Takeaways and What's Next *111*

PART 4: MAINTAINING A POSITIVE MINDSET LONG-TERM **113**

CHAPTER 14: LIFESTYLE CHANGES TO SUPPORT POSITIVE THINKING **115**

The Surprising Link Between Diet, Exercise, and Negative Thoughts *115*
Optimizing Sleep to Calm an Overactive Negative Mind *121*
Creating a Positive Environment *127*
Key Takeaways and What's Next *132*

CHAPTER 15: ADOPTING THE HABITS OF HIGHLY POSITIVE PEOPLE **135**

Understanding Positivity *135*
Characteristics and Habits of Highly Positive People *136*
Practical Steps to Adopt These Habits *137*
Your Seven-Day Challenge *139*
Key Takeaways and What's Next *139*

CHAPTER 16: NEGATIVE THOUGHT RELAPSES AND BUILDING A SUPPORT SYSTEM **141**

Understanding Negative Thought Relapses *141*

 What Is a Support System?..*145*
 Identifying and Building Your Own Support System *147*
 Benefits of Having a Strong Support System *149*
 Key Takeaways *150*

CONCLUSION 153

 THE JOURNEY SO FAR: FROM NEGATIVITY NINJA TO POSITIVITY PRO *153*
 KEY POINTS TO REMEMBER..*154*
  Understanding Negative Thinking: The Villain of Our Story *154*
  Identifying Your Negative Thought Patterns: Know Thy Enemy.................*154*
  Proven Strategies to Break Free of Negativity: Your Positivity Toolbox *155*
  Maintaining a Positive Mindset Long-Term: The Marathon, Not the Sprint
  ....*155*
  Key Takeaways: All You Can Eat Wisdom *156*
  Your Mission *157*
  A Small Favor (No Pressure, but Also Yes, Pressure) *158*
  Last Words..*158*

REFERENCES 161

Introduction: The Pervasive Problem of Negative Thinking

I'm not good enough for this job. They're going to figure out I'm a fraud any day now.

Why do I even bother trying? Nothing ever works for me, anyway.

Everyone else seems to have it all together. What's wrong with me?

I made one mistake, and now the whole project is ruined. I'm such a failure.

They didn't text back right away. They must be mad at me or don't want to be friends anymore.

Do any of these thoughts sound familiar to you? Well, you're not alone. We all have moments when negative thinking takes over, casting an awful shadow over everything in our lives. It's exhausting, I know. Those pessimistic thoughts start to overshadow everything else in your life, and soon, even the simplest tasks can feel like you're standing at the foot of Mount Everest, preparing to climb.

You're not the only person to have felt this way. More importantly, I want you to know right now that you're not doomed to stay trapped in this cycle forever. That's why I wrote this book. I want to show you that there's a way out of this thinking and a path to becoming a more positive thinker. Before you ask: No, I am not going to tell you to ignore reality and pretend that everything in your life is sunshine and rainbows when it isn't. I'm going to teach you how to work through life's challenges with a more balanced and resilient mindset.

In case you're wondering, I'm not a therapist or a neuroscientist. I'm someone who is probably a lot like you—who has been in the trenches with negative thinking, battling it day in and day out. I've spent many years researching and trying out different techniques. And yes, sometimes it hasn't always worked out. But through everything I have experienced and learned, I have been able to gather a toolkit of strategies that really do work—tried and tested, not just on myself but countless others who have shared their struggles with me.

My journey started early; I was just a kid and probably the world's tiniest pessimist. Even back then, every setback felt like the end of the world. I used to see other kids fall down and get back up with huge smiles. Not me. As I grew older, those thought patterns only seemed to get worse. It affected everything: my relationships, my career, and eventually, my health. I knew something needed to change, but I felt so stuck. I was knee-deep in quicksand, and I just needed the right leverage to get out.

I stumbled across a cognitive psychology book almost by chance. There, I learned all about positive thinking strategies and mindfulness practices. After that, I started reading every book I could get my hands on. This led me to workshops and professional help. It took time, but I began to see changes in myself. Those dark clouds in my mind didn't suddenly break up and spill sunlight. Instead, I learned how to walk around them and find the silver linings.

Later, when I started sharing my experiences with others, I began to realize just how many people struggle with the same thing. That's what inspired me to write this book. I wanted to create a resource for people like me, where they could access scientific research but with practical, real-world advice, too. I know that therapy, counseling, and other professional services can be daunting, so this book is here to bridge that gap.

If you're reading this, you can probably relate to my story, and I bet you're here because you're fed up with the negativity cycle. Well, you're in the right place! I'm not going to teach you about magical thinking or how to ignore your real-life problems. I'm going to give you some very real strategies for working on yourself to help you build your resilience and find your balance. I'm also not going to give you many other personal stories or anecdotes past this one. My goal for this book is to get right to the point so you can start changing your thinking right away.

How am I going to do that? Well...

- First, you're going to learn about the origins of negative thoughts: Where do they come from? Why do our brains seem so eager to latch onto the negative? Understanding the "why" behind your thought patterns is the first step to changing them.

- Then, you'll learn how to identify your unique negative thinking patterns and triggers. This is a bit like becoming a detective of your own mind. You'll discover how to spot those sneaky negative thoughts *before* they start to spiral out of control.

- Once you've learned to identify the problem, we'll move on to exploring proven strategies for overcoming negative thinking. I promise these won't just be quick fixes or feel-good platitudes; these are practical, science-backed techniques that you can start using right away to shift your mindset.

- Finally, because I know how tough it can be to make lasting changes, we'll also cover tips for lifestyle adjustments and long-term strategies to keep the negativity at bay. My goal isn't just to give you a temporary boost; I want to help you rewire your brain for long-lasting positivity.

Full disclosure: I am not here to promise you a life free from negative thoughts. That's not realistic, and frankly, who would really want that? Negative thoughts do have their place; they warn us about danger and can even motivate us to make positive changes. What I am going to do is help you learn how to manage those thoughts and keep them from running the show.

You've already taken the first step by picking up this book. Let's take step number two... see you in Chapter 1!

PART 1:
Understanding Negative Thinking

Chapter 1:

The Science Behind Negative Thoughts

Why are our brains sometimes hellbent on seeing the glass as half-empty, cracked, and probably poisoned? That's exactly what we're going to be covering in this chapter. There's a whole lot of science behind negative thinking. I promise I won't bore you, but it is important to understand the scientific perspective around negative thinking so you can then learn how to manage those thoughts.

What Is Negative Thinking?

Let's start with the basics. Negative thinking is more than just having a bad day or feeling a bit grumpy because someone ate the last cookie in the break room. It's a persistent pattern of thoughts that skew toward the pessimistic, the fearful, and the self-critical (Cuncic, 2020; Smith, 2022).

Here are some classic examples of negative thinking in action:

- *I messed up that presentation. I'm definitely getting fired.*

- *No one talked to me at the party. I must be boring and unlikable.*

- *My partner is late coming home. They've probably been in a terrible accident.*

Thoughts like these aren't just random occurrences. They often fall into the specific categories of negative thinking patterns. Let's break down a few of the most common ones (Harvard University, n.d.; Sage Neuroscience Center, n.d.):

- **Catastrophizing:** This is the mental equivalent of turning a paper cut into a life-threatening wound. It's when your brain takes a small problem and blows it up to apocalyptic proportions.

    o **Example:** *I forgot to reply to that email. My entire career is over!*

- **Black-and-white thinking:** Also known as all-or-nothing thinking, this is when your brain decides there are only two options: perfect or total failure. There's no room for the messy middle ground where most of life actually happens.

    o **Example:** *If I can't do this perfectly, there's no point in trying at all.*

- **Overgeneralization:** This is when your brain takes one negative event and decides it's the new rule for everything.

    o **Example:** *I went on one bad date. I'm going to be alone forever.*

- **Personalization:** This is your brain's way of making everything about you—especially the bad stuff.

    o **Example:** *The project failed. It must be all my fault.*

These patterns of thinking aren't just annoying; they can have a real impact on how we perceive the world and how we live our lives. But why do our brains do this to us? Well, this is where things get really interesting.

Biological Factors: It's Not Just All in Your Head (Well, It Is, but You Know What I Mean)

Believe it or not, our tendency toward negative thinking isn't just a personal failing or a bad habit. There's actually a biological basis for it. Yep, you read that right! Your brain might be hardwired for negativity. But before you start feeling negative about that (see what I did there?), let's break it down.

First up, let's talk about genetics. Research has shown that there's a genetic component to how we process emotions and thoughts (Bevilacqua & Goldman, 2011). Some people are more predisposed to anxiety and depression, which can fuel negative thinking patterns. It's like some of us got the deluxe worry package preinstalled at birth. But don't panic—having a genetic predisposition doesn't mean you're doomed to a life of negativity. It just means you might need to work a little harder to rewire those thought patterns.

Now, let's consider the role of hormones—particularly our old friend cortisol. Cortisol is often called the "stress hormone," and for good reason. When we're stressed, our bodies pump out cortisol like it's going out of style. This hormone can actually influence how our brains process information, making us more likely to focus on potential threats or negative outcomes (Tribby, 2022). It's like cortisol puts our brains on high alert, scanning for danger at every turn. This made a lot of sense back when we were cave-dwelling humans worried about saber-toothed tigers, but it's less helpful when we're stressing about a work presentation or a first date.

Psychological Factors: Your Brain's Favorite Tricks

Now that we've covered the biological basis, let's consider the psychological factors that contribute to negative thinking. Our brains, clever as they are, have developed a whole host of cognitive biases. These are mental shortcuts that help us process information quickly but not always accurately (Cherry, 2024).

One of the biggest culprits when it comes to negative thinking is confirmation bias. This is our brain's tendency to search for, interpret, and recall information in a way that confirms our pre-existing beliefs (Casad & Luebering, 2024). So, if you already believe you're not good enough, your brain will helpfully point out every little mistake you make while conveniently ignoring your successes. Thanks, brain!

Another major player is the negativity bias. This is our brain's tendency to give more weight to negative experiences than positive ones (Pilat & Krastev, 2021). It's why one criticism can outweigh ten compliments in our minds. From a historical standpoint, this made sense; it was more important for our ancestors to remember which berries made them sick than which ones tasted good. But in our modern world, this bias can lead us to focus disproportionately on the negative aspects of our lives.

Neuroplasticity: Your Brain's Superpower (and Sometimes Its Kryptonite)

Now, here's where things get really exciting. Our brains have this amazing ability called neuroplasticity—the capacity to change and reorganize itself by forming new neural connections (Marzola et al., 2023). It's like your brain is a never-ending construction site, constantly building new pathways and tearing down old ones.

This is fantastic news because it means we're not stuck with the brain we're born with. We can actually change our thought patterns and rewire our brains to be more positive. However, there's a catch. Just as we can train our brains to be more positive, we can also inadvertently train them to be more negative.

When we repeatedly engage in negative thinking patterns, we're essentially creating a super-highway for those thoughts in our brains. The more we use these negative pathways, the stronger and more automatic they become. It's like your brain is saying, "Oh, you want to catastrophize? No problem, I've got a direct route for that!"

This is how persistent negative thoughts can actually alter our brain structure and function over time, reinforcing that negativity bias we talked about earlier. Think of it like wearing a path through a field—the more you walk it, the more defined and easier to follow it becomes.

Key Takeaways and What's Next

Negative thinking isn't just a bad habit or a personal failure. It's a complex interplay of biological, psychological, and neurological factors. Understanding this is crucial because it takes away some of the shame and self-blame that often comes with negative thinking patterns.

Knowing that your brain might be predisposed to negativity or that you've inadvertently trained it to focus on the negative doesn't mean you're doomed to a life of pessimism. Far from it! This knowledge is actually the first step toward change—just as we can train our brains to be more negative, we can also train them to be more positive.

Later on in the book, we'll explore practical strategies for rewriting those neural pathways, managing stress hormones, and challenging those pesky cognitive biases. But before all that, we need to learn how these thought patterns feed into anxiety and stress—which is the topic for Chapter 2. We'll explore the vicious cycle of negative thoughts and anxious feelings and start to look at ways to break free from the loop.

Remember, understanding the mechanisms behind negative thinking doesn't make you weak or broken; it makes you human. More importantly, it gives you the power to change. Keep that in mind as you move through the rest of this book.

Chapter 2:

The Vicious Cycle— How Negative Thoughts Feed Anxiety and Stress

Whether you already know it or not, your negative thinking, anxiety, and stress are all tangled up together, like wired headphones left in your pocket overnight. In this chapter, we'll be looking at that connection and exploring some real-life examples so we can start figuring out how to break this toxic cycle.

In order to do that, we need to unravel the relationship between those pesky negative thoughts, the anxiety that keeps us up at night, and the stress that seems to hang over us like a cloud, blocking out the sun. It's all intertwined, and understanding this web we find ourselves in is the first step toward freeing ourselves from its grip.

The Relationship Between Negative Thoughts, Anxiety, and Stress

You're lying in bed, trying to sleep, when suddenly, your brain helpfully reminds you of that awkward thing you said at a party... five years ago. Before you know it, you're spiraling through a highlight reel of every embarrassing moment in your life, your heart's racing and sleep seems about as likely as winning the lottery without buying a ticket.

What you've just experienced is the way that negative thoughts can trigger anxiety and stress.

The question is: Why does this happen?

Well, it turns out that our thoughts, feelings, and physical responses are more interconnected than those headphones we were talking about earlier.

When we have persistent negative thoughts, our brain interprets these as threats. And what does our brain do when it perceives a threat? It sounds the alarm, triggering our body's stress response. Hello, cortisol and adrenaline! This physical stress response then reinforces the feeling that something is wrong, which—you guessed it—leads to more negative thoughts. It's like a never-ending game of ping pong, except that nobody's having fun anymore.

Now, I am not just pulling this out of thin air. The science backs this up. Studies have shown that there is a clear link between stressful life events, chronic difficulties, and symptoms of psychological distress (Muscatell et al., 2009). Likewise, Hankin et al. (2004) found that negative thinking styles could predict who was more likely to develop depression and anxiety when faced with stress.

So, if you've ever felt like your negative thoughts were making you anxious, and your anxiety was making you think more negatively... congratulations! You are not going crazy; you are simply human.

The Snowball Effect: How It All Spirals Out of Control

Now that we understand the connection, let's talk about how this can spiral faster than a toddler on a sugar high.

Meet Rayne. Rayne has a presentation at work tomorrow. As she's preparing, she thinks, *I'm going to mess this up*. This thought makes her feel anxious—her heart races, and her palms sweat. All these physical sensations make her think, *See? I'm not ready. I'm going to embarrass myself*. Now, she's even more anxious. She loses sleep that night and walks into the presentation, exhausted and jittery. She stumbles over her words and walks out thinking, *I knew I'd mess up. I'm terrible at this*.

Just like that, Rayne's negative thoughts became a self-fulfilling prophecy, reinforcing her belief that she's bad at presentations and setting her up for more anxiety next time.

Next, let's consider David. David's been single for a while and is feeling lonely. He thinks *I'm going to be alone forever.* This thought makes him feel depressed and anxious. He starts to withdraw from social situations, thinking, *Why bother? No one's interested in me anyway.* His withdrawal means he meets fewer people, which then reinforces his belief that he'll be alone forever. It's like his negative thoughts are writing a script, and he's unknowingly playing the lead role.

These aren't just hypothetical scenarios. I've heard countless stories like these from real people. Like Mercedes who told me, "I used to wake up every morning already anxious about the ways I might fail during the day. By the time I got to work, I was a ball of stress, second-guessing every decision. It was exhausting, and it made me dread each day before it even began."

Or Stephen, who shared, "My negative thoughts about my abilities at work got so bad that I started calling in sick more often. Of course, this only made me fall behind, which fueled more negative thoughts. It was like quicksand—the more I struggled, the deeper I sank."

The truth is that we've all been Rayne, David, Mercedes, or Stephen at some point. This cycle isn't a character flaw or a sign of weakness. It's a very human experience rooted in the way our brains work. But the good news is that understanding this cycle is the first step to breaking it.

The Cycle Breakdown: Your Emergency Exit Strategy

Now that you know all about this horrible cycle, let's start learning how to break it, shall we?

Just as with any kind of cycle, the key is quite simply to intervene—at any point. Remember, it's a cycle, which means you have multiple opportunities to halt its progress. Let's look at a few potential exit strategies:

- **Thought challenging:** This is about questioning your negative thoughts. Are they based on facts or feelings? Is there another way to look at the situation? We'll dive deeper into this in later chapters, but for now, just know that your thoughts aren't always telling you the truth.

- **Mindfulness:** This isn't just for Zen masters and yoga instructors. Mindfulness is about observing your thoughts and feelings without judgment. It's like watching clouds pass in the sky—you see them, but you don't have to chase them.

- **Physical relaxation:** Remember how the physical symptoms of anxiety can trigger more negative thoughts? Well, we can use this connection to our advantage. Deep breathing, progressive muscle relaxation, or even a brisk walk can help calm your body, which can, in turn, calm your mind.

- **Behavior changes:** Sometimes, to think differently, we need to act differently. This might mean facing a fear in small, manageable steps or doing something kind for yourself to challenge the negative self-talk.

These are not magic solutions that will instantly solve all your problems. If only it were that easy! These are skills, and like all skills, they take practice. The point is that you are not helpless in this cycle. You have more power than you might think to change its course.

Key Takeaways and What's Next

Negative thoughts, anxiety, and stress are interconnected, often creating a self-reinforcing cycle. But understanding this connection gives you the power to intervene. When you recognize how your thoughts influence your feelings and behaviors, and vice versa, you are already one step ahead. Suddenly, you are no longer a passenger on this joy ride; you're learning how to operate the controls.

Remember:

1. Negative thoughts can trigger anxiety and stress.

2. The physical symptoms of anxiety can then fuel more negative thoughts.

3. This can become a self-reinforcing cycle if left unchecked.

4. But you have the power to interrupt this cycle at various points.

Understanding the cycle doesn't make it magically disappear, unfortunately. But it does give you a map of the terrain you are navigating. On this journey of managing negative thinking, anxiety, and stress, having a map is a pretty big deal.

In the next chapter, we're going to start exploring the world of positive psychology and how it might just be the counterweight we need for all this negativity. Things are about to get much more optimistic around here!

Chapter 3:

Positive Psychology— The Antidote to Negativity?

Before you roll your eyes and close the book, this is not about to be one of those chapters telling you to think happy thoughts, and then all your problems will float away like balloons at a kid's birthday party. I told you before that we are not slapping a smiley face sticker over your problems here. Instead, this chapter is going to help you understand how focusing on the good stuff can actually help you deal with the bad stuff better.

We're going to learn what positive psychology actually is (and it's not just being annoyingly cheerful all the time), why it matters, and how you can use it in your everyday life without feeling like you're starring in a cheesy self-help infomercial. We're also going to look at some real-life success stories, check out what the science says, and even give you a chance to try out some techniques yourself.

What Is Positive Psychology?

Positive psychology is not about ignoring the negative stuff in life or pretending that everything's peachy keen when it's clearly not. It's a branch of psychology that focuses on what makes life worth living rather than just what goes wrong.

You can think of traditional psychology as the mechanic trying to fix a broken-down car, whereas positive psychology is more like a driving instructor teaching you how to navigate the roads more skilfully, even when there are potholes and crazy drivers everywhere.

This field kicked off around the turn of the millennium when a psychologist named Martin Seligman decided that psychology spent too much time focusing on what was wrong with people and not enough on what was right (Gibbon, 2020). He decided to study happy, well-adjusted people and see what makes them tick. It was like studying healthy people to figure out how to avoid getting sick instead of just studying sick people to figure out how to cure them.

Positive psychology differs from traditional approaches in a few key ways:

1. It focuses on strengths, not just weaknesses.

2. It aims to build the good in life, not just repair the bad.

3. It's interested in making the lives of all people better, not just treating mental illness.

In other words, it's not about fixing what's broken but nurturing what's already working.

The Importance of Positive Psychology

Right now, you might be wondering how focusing on positive psychology is going to help you when life keeps throwing lemons at your head.

Well, focusing on your strengths rather than your weaknesses is like working out the muscles you already have instead of just worrying about the flab. It makes you stronger, more resilient, and better equipped to handle life's challenges.

Think about it this way: When you're facing a tough situation, what's more helpful—obsessing over everything that could go wrong or remembering times when you've successfully overcome challenges in the past?

Positive psychology helps you build up a reservoir of good experiences and emotions that you can draw on when times get tough. It's not about ignoring the negative but about building up your psychological immune system so you can bounce back faster when life knocks you down. It helps you build your resilience, strengthen your coping mechanisms, and improve your overall well-being.

How to Apply Positive Psychology Principles

So, how do you actually use positive psychology in everyday life? Let's look at a few key principles and how to apply them:

- **Gratitude:** This isn't just about saying "thanks" when someone holds the door open. The key is to regularly acknowledge the good things in your life, whether they are big or small. Try keeping a gratitude journal. Each day, write down three things you're grateful for. They can be as simple as "my morning coffee" or as profound as "my supportive partner."

- **Optimism:** This doesn't mean expecting everything to always work out perfectly. It's about looking for opportunities during challenges and believing in your ability to handle whatever comes your way. When you face a setback, try asking yourself, "What can I learn from this?" or "How might this be an opportunity in disguise?"

- **Mindfulness:** This is about being present in the moment rather than worrying about the future or dwelling on the past. Try this quick mindfulness exercise: Stop what you're doing and focus on your breath for one minute. Pay attention to the sensation of the air moving in and out of your body. If you notice your mind wandering, gently bring your attention back to your breath.

- **Strengths:** Instead of obsessing over your weaknesses, identify and lean into your strengths. Take a moment to write down five things you're good at—they can be skills, personality traits, or anything you consider a personal strength.

Don't forget that these aren't one-and-done solutions. They're skills that need to be practiced regularly, like exercising a muscle. The more you do them, the stronger and more automatic they become. We will be exploring some of these in more depth later on in the book.

Case Studies Relating to Positive Psychology

Yes, this all sounds good on paper, but does it actually work in real life? Well, let me introduce you to Alexis and Mo.

Alexis was a chronic worrier. She'd lie awake at night cataloging everything that could possibly go wrong the next day, week, or decade. She decided to try keeping a gratitude journal. At first, she felt silly writing things down like "my comfy bed" or "the sound of birds in the morning." But after a few weeks, she noticed something strange; she was starting to look forward to her journaling time. More than that, she found herself noticing good things throughout the day, almost like her brain was collecting material for her journal. Six months in, Alexis still has worries, but she finds them easier to manage. "It's like I've trained my brain to look for the good stuff," she says. "The worries are still there, but they're not the only thing I see anymore."

Then there's Mo. Mo had always been a glass-half-empty kind of guy. After a particularly rough patch in his life, he decided to try practicing optimism. He started small, just trying to find one positive aspect in challenging situations. It felt forced at first but gradually became more natural. The turning point came when he got passed over for a promotion at work. Instead of spiraling into self-doubt, he asked himself what he could learn from the experience. This led to a productive conversation with his boss about areas for improvement, and six months later, Mo not only got the promotion but felt more confident in his abilities than ever before.

Scientific Research to Support Positive Psychology

Before you start accusing me of writing a bunch of feel-good fluff, let's take a look at the science behind these smiles.

Seligman et al. (2005) found that certain optimism exercises, like writing about a time when you were at your best, could help alleviate depressive symptoms for up to six months. That's right—writing about your strengths could have a longer-lasting effect than some antidepressants!

Then, Barbara Fredrickson and her team showed that practicing loving-kindness meditation—a technique that focuses on cultivating feelings of warmth and care toward ourselves and others—could increase people's daily experiences of positive emotions (Fredrickson et al., 2008). These increased positive emotions led to increases in mindfulness, sense of purpose, and social support, all of which are crucial factors in mental health and well-being.

Speaking of mindfulness, a meta-analysis published in 2018 (Goldberg et al., 2018) looked at 142 studies on mindfulness-based interventions and found that these practices were effective in reducing anxiety, depression, and stress. The analysis showed that mindfulness was about as effective as other existing treatments, including cognitive behavioral therapy. This means that taking a few minutes a day to focus on the present moment could be as powerful as some traditional psychological treatments in managing negative thinking.

The takeaway here is that this is not just feel-good fluff; there is hard science backing up the benefits of positive psychology techniques. And remember, it is not about ignoring the negative; it's about actively cultivating the positive to build resilience and improve your overall mental health.

Key Takeaways and What's Next

Positive psychology isn't about achieving instant happiness or never feeling negative emotions again. The goal is to gradually shift your focus and build up your psychological resources.

In the next chapter, we're going to explore the hidden costs of negative thinking. We'll look at how persistent negativity can impact not just your mental health but your physical health, relationships, and overall quality of life.

Your Homework (Don't Worry, It's the Fun Kind)

Okay, students, here's your assignment. I want you to try incorporating one positive psychology technique into your life this week. Maybe it's starting a gratitude journal, trying that one-minute mindfulness exercise, or identifying one of your strengths each day.

Much like when you start going to the gym, you're not going to see massive differences after one session, but if you stick with it, you'll start noticing a difference.

If you try something that doesn't work for you, that's okay! Not every technique will resonate with every person. The key is to experiment and find what works for you.

Chapter 4:

The Hidden Costs of Chronic Negative Thinking

It's time to pull back the curtain on the sneaky, behind-the-scenes damage that chronic negative thinking can do. That voice in the back of your head that's always predicting doom and gloom isn't just annoying; it's potentially harmful in ways you might not even realize.

Chronic negative thinking can severely impact various aspects of daily life. It can affect relationships, work performance, and overall mental health. Take relationships, for example. If you constantly think your partner is going to leave you or that you are unlovable, you may become clingy or withdrawn. This behavior can push friends and family away. The ongoing fear of abandonment can reinforce the belief that you are not deserving of love, creating a vicious cycle.

In the workplace, chronic negative thinking may cause you to struggle to meet deadlines or work collaboratively with others. If you often think, *I'll never get this right*, you might procrastinate and avoid tasks. This can lead to missed opportunities for growth or recognition. A negative mindset can also lead to burnout. When you are constantly stressed and worried, it can be exhausting and drain motivation and energy.

In this chapter, we're going to take a close look at the hidden costs of letting that Negative Nancy in your head run the show. We're going to talk about physical health, mental well-being, relationships, career, and even your ability to grow as a person.

Negative thinking patterns are incredibly common in our society. We're bombarded with bad news 24-7, social media has us constantly comparing our behind-the-scenes to everyone else's highlight reel, and let's face it: it feels good at the moment, but if you do it too much, you're going to end up with some damage.

The Physical Costs of Chronic Negative Thinking

Okay, pop quiz: Do you think your thoughts are related to your physical health?

...

If you answered "nothing," I hate to break it to you, but you might want to think again. It turns out that what goes on in your head can have a pretty big impact on what goes on in the rest of your body.

Let's start with the heart—and I am not talking about heartbreak. Studies have found that people with higher levels of pessimism had a higher risk of death from heart disease (Kubzansky et al., 2001). That's right, being a half-glass-empty kind of person might actually be bad for your ticker!

There's more: Chronic negative thinking can also mess with your immune system. It's like your body's defense force decides to take a coffee break right when the invaders are at the gate. Studies have found that chronic stress (which often goes hand-in-hand with negative thinking) can suppress your immune system's ability to fight off antigens (Cohen et al., 2012). In other words, all that worrying might actually make you more likely to catch that cold going around the office.

Let's not forget about sleep. If you've ever laid awake at night, your mind racing with worst-case scenarios, you know that negative thinking and good sleep don't exactly go hand-in-hand. Chronic sleep deprivation can lead to all sorts of health issues, from weight gain to increased risk of diabetes and cardiovascular disease.

So what's the takeaway here? Your body is listening to your thoughts. Maybe it's time to start saying nice things about it!

The Mental Health Impact

Now, let's talk about what's going on upstairs. You might think that negative thinking only affects your mood, but the reality is that it goes much deeper than that.

Chronic negative thinking is like letting a termite infestation loose in the structure of your mental health. At first, you might not notice much damage, but give it time, and things can really start to crumble.

A strong link has been found between rumination (that's psychology-speak for repetitive negative thinking) and an increased risk of depression and anxiety (Olatunji et al., 2013). It's like your brain gets stuck in a negative thought loop, and the more it goes around, the deeper the groove becomes, making it harder and harder to jump out.

It's not just about feeling sad or worried. Chronic negative thinking can actually change the way your brain functions. Studies have shown that people who engage in a lot of negative self-talk tend to have increased activity in the amygdala, the part of your brain responsible for the fight-or-flight response (Frewen et al., 2008). Essentially, your brain starts treating everyday situations like life-or-death emergencies. That sounds exhausting, doesn't it?

Finally, chronic stress, which is often fueled by negative thinking, can actually shrink your brain. Specifically, it can reduce the size of the hippocampus, which plays a crucial role in learning and memory (Sapolsky, 2000). So not only does negative thinking make you *feel* bad, but it might also make you less sharp.

Relationship Strains and Professional Setbacks Due to Negative Thinking

We're going to dive deeper into these topics in future chapters, but I'd be remiss if I didn't at least touch on how chronic negativity can impact your relationships and career.

Think about it: Would you want to hang out with someone who's constantly complaining and always seeing the worst in every situation? Probably not, right? Well, guess what? Other people feel the same way. Chronic negativity can be a real buzzkill, and over time, it can strain even the strongest relationships. It's like emotional vampire syndrome, and you're unwittingly sucking the joy out of your interactions with others.

When it comes to your career, negative thinking can be a real roadblock. It can hold you back from taking risks, pursuing opportunities, or even just performing at your best. After all, if you're constantly telling yourself you're going to fail, you're a lot less likely to put in the effort to succeed. It's like sabotaging yourself before you even get started.

We'll explore these in more depth later on, but for now, just keep in mind that the impacts of negative thinking can ripple out far beyond your inner world.

How Negative Thinking Can Limit Personal Growth and Happiness

Negative thinking can, unfortunately, become your own personal dream-squashing machine if you let it. You know those big, exciting goals you have? You know, those goals that make your heart race a little when you think about them? Well, chronic negative thinking is like kryptonite to those dreams. It's that voice in the back of your head that says, "Who do you think you are?" or "You'll probably just fail anyway, so why bother?"

This constant barrage of pessimism can lead to something psychologists call "learned helplessness." It's when you've convinced yourself that you have no control over your circumstances, so you stop trying to change them. It's like training yourself to stay in a jail cell even when the door is wide open.

It goes beyond just holding you back from big achievements. Negative thinking can rob you of everyday jobs and small victories, too. When you're always focused on what could go wrong, you miss out on appreciating what's going right. It's like walking through a beautiful garden and only noticing the weeds.

Research has shown that people who engage in more positive thinking tend to be more resilient, more successful, and, yes, happier overall (Taherkhani et al., 2023). They're more likely to try new things, bounce back from setbacks, and see opportunities where others see obstacles.

How many opportunities have you talked yourself out of because you were sure you would fail? How many potentially amazing experiences have you missed because you were too focused on all the things that could go wrong?

The cost of chronic negative thinking isn't just in what it does to you; it's in what it prevents you from doing, experiencing, and becoming.

Key Takeaways and What's Next

We've seen how chronic negative thinking can impact your physical health, your mental well-being, your relationships, your career, and your personal growth. It's a lot to take in, I know. It isn't meant to be all doom and gloom. This is a wake-up call. It's a spotlight on an issue that many of us don't even realize causes so much havoc in our lives. The good news is that once you're aware of these hidden costs, you can start doing something about them.

Remember:

- Chronic negative thinking can have serious impacts on your physical health, including an increased risk of heart disease and a weakened immune system.

- Your mental health takes a big hit from constant negativity, with increased risks of depression, anxiety, and other stress-related disorders.

- Negative thinking can strain your relationships and hold you back in your career.

- Perhaps most insidiously, chronic pessimism can limit your personal growth and rob you of happiness by keeping you from pursuing opportunities and appreciating the good things in life.

- The costs of negative thinking go far beyond just feeling bad; they can impact every area of your life.

Now that you're aware of the hidden costs of chronic negative thinking, you're in a better position to start shifting toward a more balanced, positive outlook.

If you're wondering how to actually change your thinking patterns, you're in luck because that's exactly what we're going to start exploring in the next chapter. We'll be looking at the most common types of negative thinking traps and how to spot them in your own thought processes.

PART 2:
Identifying Your Negative Thought Patterns

Chapter 5:

The 7 Most Common Negative Thinking Traps and Discovering Your Unique "Negativity Fingerprint"

Negative thinking traps—sounds mysterious, doesn't it? In this chapter, we're going to explore the seven most common negative thinking traps that snare us at one time or another. These are the usual suspects in the lineup of mental mishaps. We'll also learn how to identify which of these traps you tend to fall into most often, creating your unique negativity fingerprint. It's like CSI for your mind!

By the end of the chapter, you'll be able to spot these sneaky thought patterns from a mile away. Let's get to know your enemy, shall we?

The 7 Most Common Negative Thinking Traps

We touched on some of these earlier on, but here are the seven most common negative thinking traps (Naoumidis, 2019; Touroni, 2022):

All-Or-Nothing Thinking: The Perfectionist's Pitfall

This is the trap of extremes. You're either a complete success or a total failure. There's no middle ground, no room for partial victories or learning experiences.

Real-life example: Amber worked hard on a project at work. Her boss praised her overall but suggested a few minor changes. Amber's immediate thought was: *I'm a complete failure. I can't do anything right.*

Overgeneralization: When One Bad Apple Spoils the Whole Bunch

This is when you take one negative event and turn it into a never-ending pattern of defeat.

Real-life example: Aaron asked someone out on a date and got turned down. His immediate conclusion was: *I'll never find love. I'm going to be alone forever.*

Mental Filter: Focusing on the One Dark Cloud in a Sunny Sky

This trap involves focusing solely on the negative details of a situation while ignoring all the positives.

Real-life example: Lisa got mostly positive feedback on her presentation, but one person looked bored. Lisa can't stop thinking about that one person, completely discounting all the positive reactions.

Disqualifying the Positive: The "Yes, But" Syndrome

This is the habit of dismissing positive experiences by insisting they "don't count" for some reason or other.

Real-life example: Marco's friend compliments him on his guitar playing. Marco's immediate response is: "Oh, it's nothing. Anyone could do it if they practiced enough."

Jumping to Conclusions: The Fortune Teller's Folly

This trap involves making negative interpretations without actual evidence. It comes in two flavors:

- **Mind reading:** Assuming you know what people are thinking.
- **Fortune telling:** Predicting that things will turn out badly.

Real-life example: Emma hasn't heard from her friend in a few days. She concludes: *She must be mad at me. Our friendship is probably over.*

Magnification (Catastrophizing) or Minimization: The Broken Binoculars

This involves exaggerating the importance of negative events or minimizing the importance of positive ones.

Real-life example: Faizan makes a small mistake at work. His mind immediately jumps to: *I'm going to get fired, lose my house, and end up living on the street.*

Emotional Reasoning: Feeling Your Way to Faulty Conclusions

This is the belief that because you feel something, it must be true.

Real-life example: Rachel feels anxious about flying. She thinks: *I feel scared, so flying must be dangerous.*

How to Identify Which Trap(s) You Frequently Fall Into

Now that we've met our suspects, it's time to figure out which ones are lurking in your mental alleyways. This is where things get personal—and a bit tricky. After all, these thought patterns can be sneaky little devils, often disguising themselves as "just being realistic" or "preparing for the worst."

So, how do we catch them in the act? Enter mindfulness.

Mindfulness is all about paying attention to the present moment without judgment. It's like setting up a security camera in your mind, allowing you to observe your thoughts as they come and go. Let me tell you, it can be quite an eye-opener!

In the book *Mindfulness-Based Cognitive Therapy for Depression, First Edition: A New Approach to Preventing Relapse* (Segal et al., 2002), it was shown that practicing mindfulness can help people become more aware of their thought patterns, including those pesky negative ones. It's like turning on the lights in a dark room—suddenly, you can see all the stuff you've been tripping over.

Here's a quick mindfulness exercise to get you started:

1. Find a quiet moment and sit comfortably.

2. Close your eyes and take a few deep breaths.

3. Notice your thoughts as they come and go without trying to change them.

4. If you notice a negative thought, try to identify which of the seven traps it might fall into.

5. Don't judge yourself for having the thought—just observe it.

Try this for a few minutes each day, and you'll notice patterns emerging. Which brings us to...

Your Unique "Negativity Fingerprint"

Just like your actual fingerprint, your negativity fingerprint is uniquely yours. It's the particular combination of negative thinking traps that you tend to fall into most often. Some people might be champion catastrophizers with a side of mental filtering, while others might specialize in all-or-nothing thinking with a dash of overgeneralization.

Recognizing your negativity fingerprint is like having a personalized map of your mental pitfalls. It can help you understand why certain situations trigger stress or anxiety for you. For instance, if your fingerprint includes a lot of fortune-telling, you might find yourself particularly anxious about future events. If disqualifying the positive is your thing, you might struggle with self-esteem issues.

To identify your negativity fingerprint, try keeping a thought journal for a week. When you notice yourself feeling anxious, stressed, or down, jot down your thoughts and see which traps they fall into. Look for patterns: Which traps show up most often? In what situations?

This is not about judging yourself or feeling bad about your thought patterns. It's simply about gaining awareness first so you can begin to change them.

Practical Strategies to Overcome Each Trap

Let's take a brief look at some strategies for combating each trap. These are just starting points; we're going to dive deeper into techniques in later chapters.

- **All-or-nothing thinking**

    - **Strategy:** Practice finding the middle ground. Ask yourself, "Is there a less extreme way to look at this?"

    - **Example:** Instead of "I'm a complete failure," try "I did some things well, and there's room for improvement in others."

- **Overgeneralization**

    - **Strategy:** Look for evidence that contradicts your generalization.

    - **Example:** When thinking, *I never succeed*, remember your past successes, no matter how small.

- **Mental filter**

    - **Strategy:** Consciously acknowledge the positives, if your mind wants to focus on the negatives.

- **Example:** For every negative you notice, challenge yourself to find two positives.

- **Disqualifying the positive**
  - **Strategy:** Practice accepting compliments instead of deflecting them.
  - **Example:** Instead of, "Oh, it was nothing," try "Thank you. I'm glad you enjoyed it."

- **Jumping to conclusions**
  - **Strategy:** Treat your negative predictions as hypotheses, not facts. Look for evidence.
  - **Example:** Instead of assuming a friend is mad at you, ask yourself, "What evidence do I have for this? Could there be other explanations?"

- **Magnification or minimization**
  - **Strategy:** Use the "Will this matter in 5 years?" test to gain perspective.
  - **Example:** When catastrophizing, ask yourself how likely the worst-case scenario really is.

- **Emotional reasoning**
  - **Strategy:** Remind yourself that feelings aren't facts. Use the phrase, "I feel X, but that doesn't necessarily mean Y."
  - **Example:** "I feel anxious about this presentation, but that doesn't mean I'm going to fail."

Overcoming these thinking traps takes practice, so be patient with yourself as you learn to recognize and challenge these patterns. There are plenty more tips and suggestions coming up to complement these strategies and your growth.

Key Takeaways and What's Next

Let's recap what we've learned in this chapter:

- There are seven common negative thinking traps that we all fall into from time to time.

- Mindfulness can be a powerful tool for identifying these traps in your own thinking.

- Your negativity fingerprint is your unique combination of these traps, and recognizing it can help you understand your personal stress and anxiety triggers better.

- These patterns are habits, not character flaws. Like any habit, they can be changed with awareness and practice.

The next chapter is going to take us into the world of negative self-talk and the stories we tell ourselves. We'll explore how these internal narratives shape our reality and learn how to rewrite them.

Chapter 6:

Negative Self-Talk and the Stories We Tell Ourselves

Do you have an annoying little voice in your head? That inner critic who's always ready with a snappy put-down or a gloomy prediction?

Welcome to the not-so-wonderful world of negative self-talk.

Negative self-talk is that pesky internal dialogue that undermines your confidence, amplifies your fears, and turns molehills into mountains. It doesn't just make you feel bad; it can also significantly ramp up your stress and anxiety levels.

In this chapter, we're going to dive deep into the rabbit hole of our internal dialogue. We'll explore what negative self-talk actually is, the different flavors it comes in, and how it shapes the stories we tell ourselves about, well, ourselves.

Don't worry; I'm not here just to point out the problem. I'm also going to teach you some tricks to change the channel on that negative broadcast. This might be the most important conversation you'll ever have—the one you have with yourself.

What Is Negative Self-Talk?

Negative self-talk is not just when you're having a bad day or when you occasionally think, *Ugh, I'm such an idiot*, when you forget your keys. Negative self-talk is a pattern of self-directed thoughts that are overly critical, pessimistic, or downright mean. The seminal work *Cognitive Therapy of Depression* (Beck et al., 1987) describes these negative thoughts as automatic, repetitive, and often distorted views of oneself, the world, and the future. It's like having a tiny, grumpy drill sergeant living in your head, always ready to point out your flaws and shortcomings.

This inner dialogue can actually shape our emotions and behaviors. When we constantly tell ourselves we're not good enough, smart enough, or worthy enough, we start to believe it. And when we start to believe it, we act accordingly. Beck and his colleagues argue that these negative thought patterns play a crucial role in the development and maintenance of emotional disorders, particularly depression (Beck et al., 1987). It's like a self-fulfilling prophecy, but not the fun kind where you predict you'll win the lottery.

Types of Negative Self-Talk

Negative self-talk isn't a one-size-fits-all kind of deal. It comes in different flavors, each with its own special way of making you feel lousy. Let's meet the four main types (Beau, 2021; Sutton, 2020). You may recognize these from the previous chapter, but they make their way into our self-talk, too!:

- **Personalizing:** This is the "it's all my fault" type of thinking. You blame yourself for everything that goes wrong, even when it's not remotely your fault.

    - **Example:** Your friend is in a bad mood, and you immediately think, *What did I do wrong?*

- **Magnifying:** Also known as catastrophizing, this is when you blow things way out of proportion.

    - **Example:** You make a small mistake at work and think, *I'm going to get fired, and I'll never find another job!*

- **Catastrophizing:** This is like magnifying on steroids. You always expect the worst possible outcome.

- - **Example:** You have a slight headache and immediately conclude that it must be a brain tumor.

- **Polarizing:** This is also called black-and-white thinking. It is when you see things in extreme terms with no middle ground.

  - **Example:** If you're not perfect at something, you consider yourself a total failure.

Recognizing these patterns is the first step to changing them. It's like being able to name the monster under your bed—somehow, it becomes a little less scary.

The Stories We Tell Ourselves

Here's where things get really interesting: All this negative self-talk is not just random thoughts. Over time, it weaves itself into the stories we tell ourselves about who we are, what we're capable of, and what we deserve.

In his book *Rewire Your Brain: Think Your Way to a Better Life*, John B. Arden (2010) talks about how these internal narratives shape our perception of reality. It's like we're all walking around with our own personal Hollywood screenwriter in our heads, constantly crafting and revising the story of our lives.

The problem is that when that screenwriter is feeling particularly negative, the stories can turn into real downers. We might craft narratives like "I'm not good enough," "I always mess things up," or "I don't deserve success." The scary part is that we start to believe these stories. We act as if they're true, which only reinforces them further.

The good news is that just like any story, these narratives can be rewritten. You might not be able to fire that inner screenwriter, but you can certainly give them some new direction.

Changing Our Narratives

Now it's time for the fun part: learning how to change these negative stories into more positive, realistic ones. Here are a few strategies to get you started:

- **Catch and check:** Start by simply noticing your negative self-talk. If you catch yourself having a negative thought, pause and ask, "Is this really true? What evidence do I have for and against this thought?"

- **Reframe the situation:** Try to look at the situation from a different perspective. What would you say to a friend in the same situation?

- **Use "and" instead of "but":** When acknowledging a negative, add a positive. Instead of "I made a mistake, but at least I learned something," try "I made a mistake, and I learned something."

- **Practice self-compassion:** Talk to yourself like you would to a good friend—with kindness and understanding.

As promised, here are a couple of exercises to help you put these strategies into practice:

Exercise 1: The Daily Thought Record

Keep a journal for a week. Each day, write down:

- Situation: What happened?

- Automatic thought: What went through your mind?

- Emotion: How did you feel?

- Alternative thought: Can you think of a more balanced or positive way to view the situation?

Exercise 2: The Self-Compassion Letter

Write a letter to yourself from the perspective of a loving, compassionate friend. What would they say about your strengths, your efforts, and your inherent worth as a person?

Key Takeaways and What's Next

Let's recap what we've learned in this chapter:

- Negative self-talk is more than just being hard on yourself; it's a pattern of thinking that can shape your emotions and behaviors.

- There are four main types of negative self-talk: personalizing, magnifying, catastrophizing, and polarizing.

- These patterns of negative self-talk create the stories we tell ourselves about who we are and what we're capable of.

- We have the power to change these narratives through strategies like catching and checking our thoughts, reframing situations, and practicing self-compassion.

Now that we've tackled the voice inside our own heads, it's time to start looking outward. In the next chapter, we'll explore how we absorb negativity from others and what we can do about it. Because, let's face it, sometimes the world around us can be just as pessimistic as our inner critic.

Chapter 7:

Absorbing Negativity From Others

Have you ever walked into a room full of grumpy people and suddenly felt your mood plummet faster than a lead balloon? Or have you spent time with a Negative Nancy and soon found yourself seeing the world through gray-tinted glasses? These are examples of how negativity can be contagious!

In this chapter, we're going to explore how we unwittingly become sponges for other people's negativity. We'll learn to recognize the sources of this external doom and gloom, discover techniques to shield ourselves from this emotional onslaught, and figure out how to deal with the Debbie Downers in our lives without turning into one ourselves.

What Is Emotional Contagion? The Science of Catching Feelings

You've probably heard the phrase "misery loves company," but did you know there's actually scientific evidence to back this up?

Emotional contagion is "the tendency to automatically mimic and synchronize facial expressions, vocalizations, postures, and movements with those of another person, and consequently, to converge emotionally" (Lin et al., 2024). In simpler terms, it's how we "catch" the emotions of others, often without even realizing it.

This concept isn't just anecdotal; it's backed by solid scientific research. A comprehensive review by Wróbel and Imbir (2019) found that this phenomenon occurs through a complex interplay of neurological, physiological, and social factors.

Here's how it works: When we observe someone expressing an emotion, our brain activates the same neural networks associated with that emotion in ourselves. It's like our brains have their own little mirror, reflecting the emotional states of those around us. This process happens rapidly and often unconsciously, which is why you might suddenly find yourself feeling down after scrolling through a feed of negative news, even if none of it directly affected you.

It's not just about mimicry. We often absorb the moods and attitudes of those around us in more subtle ways, too. Ferrara and Yang (2015) found that emotions can spread through social networks, both online and offline. Happy friends make you more likely to be happy, while connections to depressed individuals can increase your own risk of developing depressive symptoms.

This absorption of others' emotional states can be particularly potent with negative emotions. Research has shown that negative emotions tend to be more "contagious" than positive ones (Pinilla et al., 2020). It's like negativity is the emotional equivalent of a catchy pop song—it gets stuck in your head whether you want it to or not!

Understanding this concept of emotional contagion is crucial because it helps explain why we sometimes feel emotions that don't seem to have a clear cause. It's not just you being moody or oversensitive; you might genuinely be picking up on and absorbing the emotional states of those around you.

So, the next time you find yourself inexplicably grumpy after spending time with your perpetually pessimistic cousin, you're not imagining things. You've literally caught a case of the grumps!

Identifying Sources of External Negativity

Now that we know negativity can spread like wildfire, let's talk about how to spot the sources of this emotional arson in our lives.

Negative influences can come in many forms. Sometimes, they're obvious, like that coworker who always has something to complain about or that friend who can find the cloud in every silver lining. But sometimes, the source of negativity can be sneakier.

Here are some common negative ninjas to watch out for:

- **The chronic complainer:** This persona has elevated whining to an art form. Nothing is ever good enough, and they always have something to grumble about.

- **The drama magnet:** Their life is a constant soap opera, and they always need to rope you into their latest crisis.

- **The pessimistic prognosticator:** This person can predict doom and gloom in any situation. Planning a picnic? They'll tell you it's definitely going to rain.

- **The energy vampire:** After spending time with this person, you feel drained, even if you can't pinpoint why.

- **The toxic environment:** Sometimes, it's not a person but a place. A high-stress workplace or a chaotic home environment can be a breeding ground for negativity.

Let me share a story about Robin, a friend of mine. Robin couldn't figure out why she always felt anxious and irritable after her weekly lunch with her friend Jessica. On the surface, Jessica seemed nice enough. But as we dug deeper, Robin realized that Jessica had a habit of subtly putting others down and always steered the conversation toward negative topics., Jessica was a sneaky negative ninja, and Robin was absorbing all that pessimism without even realizing it.

The key is to start paying attention to how you feel after interacting with certain people or spending time in certain environments. If you consistently feel drained, anxious, or negative, you might have spotted a source of toxic negativity in your life.

Protecting Yourself From Absorbing Negativity

So, how do we protect ourselves from absorbing other people's negativity? You can think of this as building your very own emotional force field (Feeney & Collins, 2015; Lischetzke & Eid, 2017; Renner et al., 2019):

- **Set clear boundaries:** This is your first line of defense. It's okay to limit your time with negative people or to steer conversations away from constant complaining. Setting healthy boundaries in relationships is crucial for maintaining our own well-being.

- **Practice emotional distancing:** This doesn't mean becoming cold or unfeeling. It's about recognizing that you can empathize with someone's emotions without taking them on as your own. Imagine there's a glass wall between you and the other person's negativity—you can see it, but it doesn't have to touch you.

- **Engage in mood-boosting activities:** After exposure to negativity, intentionally do something that lifts your spirits. This could be exercise, listening to upbeat music, or engaging in a hobby you enjoy. Engaging in positive activities can effectively counteract negative moods.

- **Practice gratitude:** Regularly focusing on the positive aspects of your life can create a buffer against external negativity. Keep a gratitude journal or share three good things that happened each day with a friend or a family member.

- **Visualization techniques:** Imagine yourself surrounded by a protective bubble that deflects negativity. It might sound a bit crazy at first, but visualization can be a powerful tool. Positive mental imagery can significantly improve mood and reduce anxiety.

Here's a quick exercise to get you started:

The Negativity Shield Visualization

1. Find a quiet place and close your eyes.

2. Take a few deep breaths to center yourself.

3. Imagine a bright, protective light surrounding your body.

4. Visualize this light as a shield, deflecting any negative energy that comes your way.

5. When you encounter negativity, picture it bouncing off your shield.

6. Take a deep breath and open your eyes, carrying the feeling of protection with you.

Practice this visualization regularly, especially before entering situations where you might encounter negativity.

Managing Relationships With Negative Individuals

Sometimes, we can't completely avoid negative people. Maybe it's a family member, a coworker, or a long-time friend going through a rough patch. So, how do we manage these relationships without letting their negativity seep into our own psyche?

- **Set the tone:** Start conversations on a positive note. Share something good that happened to you or ask them about something positive in their life. This can help steer the interaction in a more upbeat direction.

- **Use the redirect and reframe technique:** When they start spiraling into negativity, gently redirect the conversation. If they're complaining about work, you might say, "That sounds tough. What's one small thing you could do to improve the situation?" This acknowledges their feelings while nudging them toward problem-solving.

- **Practice compassionate detachment:** Recognize that their negativity is about them and not you. You can be supportive without taking on their emotional state. It's like being a sturdy dock for a boat in stormy waters—you provide support without getting tossed about yourself.

- **Know when to step back:** If someone's negativity is persistent and starts affecting your own well-being, it's okay to create some distance. This doesn't mean ending the relationship, but it might mean limiting your interactions or setting firmer boundaries.

- **Model positive behavior:** Sometimes, the best way to deal with negativity is to consistently model a more positive outlook. Your optimism might just be contagious, too!

It's really important to remember that you are not responsible for fixing someone else's negative outlook. Your job is to manage your own emotional state and set healthy boundaries.

Key Takeaways and What's Next

In this chapter, we've learned the following:

- Emotional contagion is real; we can "catch" the moods and attitudes of those around us, especially the negative ones.

- How to identify different sources of negativity in your life, including people and environments.

- How to build your emotional force field through techniques like setting boundaries, emotional distancing, and engaging in mood-boosting activities.

- When dealing with persistently negative people, use strategies like redirection, compassionate detachment, and modeling positive behavior.

- It's not your job to fix others but to manage your own emotional well-being.

Now that we've learned how to shield ourselves from external negativity, it's time to turn our attention to one of the most powerful tools in our positivity arsenal. In the next chapter, we'll explore the "thought replacement" technique—a game-changing strategy for conquering those pesky negative thoughts that pop up in our own minds.

PART 3:
Proven Strategies to Break Free of Negativity

Chapter 8:

The "Thought Replacement" Technique for Conquering Negative Thoughts

We've spent the last two parts of this book unmasking those sneaky negative thoughts and learning how they weasel their way into our minds. Now, it's time to fight back with a superhero move of cognitive behavioral therapy: the thought replacement technique.

You can think of thought replacement as a mental makeover for your brain. It's like catching that pessimistic parrot on your shoulder mid-squawk and teaching it to sing a different tune.

In this chapter, we're going to learn the science and practice of this game-changing technique.

Understanding Thought Replacement

So, what exactly is thought replacement? In simple terms, it's the practice of consciously substituting negative thoughts with more positive, realistic ones (Fritscher, 2023). Again, it is not about slapping a smiley face sticker on your problems but rather about challenging those automatic negative thoughts and replacing them with more balanced, helpful ones.

Thought replacement is a key player in the world of cognitive behavioral therapy (CBT). CBT works by changing your thoughts to change your feelings and behaviors. It's like being your own mental personal trainer, coaching your brain to flex those positivity muscles.

The goal here isn't to eliminate negative thoughts entirely (let's face it; we're humans, not robots) but to break the cycle of negative thinking that can lead to stress, anxiety, and depression. It's about giving your brain a new script to work from, one that's more in line with reality and more conducive to your mental health.

The Science Behind Thought Replacement

It all sounds great, right? But does it actually work? Let's look at the science.

A meta-analysis by Hofmann et al. (2012) found that CBT techniques like thought replacement are effective for a wide range of mental health issues, including depression, anxiety disorders, and even some medical conditions with psychological components. It's the Swiss Army knife for your mind!

There's more: In 2006, Butler et al. reviewed meta-analyses and found that CBT is not only effective but that its effects tend to be long-lasting. It's not just a quick fix but a lasting change.

So, how does it actually change the brain?

Well, research on neuroplasticity (the brain's ability to reorganize itself) found that practices like thought replacement can actually change our brain patterns over time (Davidson & McEwen, 2012). Your brain is like a garden and thought replacement is you deciding to plant flowers instead of letting the weeds take over. With consistent practice, you are literally rewiring your brain for more positive thinking.

Implementing Thought Replacement

Okay, that's enough science talk—let's learn how to actually do it. Here's your step-by-step guide:

1. **Identify the thought:** This is where all the work we did in earlier chapters comes in handy. Catch that negative thought red-handed.

A. **Example:** *I'm going to mess up this presentation, and everyone will think I'm incompetent.*

2. **Challenge the thought:** Put on your detective hat and examine the evidence. Is this thought based on facts or feelings?

    A. **Example:** *Have I actually messed up every presentation I've ever given? No. I've done well in the past.*

3. **Replace the thought:** Now, create a more balanced, realistic thought to replace the negative one.

    A. **Example:** I've prepared well for this presentation. *Even if it's not perfect, it doesn't define my competence.*

Let's put this into practice with a quick exercise:

Thought Replacement in Action

Think of a recent negative thought you've had. Write it down. Now, go through the three steps above with this thought. What's your new replacement thought?

Remember, this isn't about forcing positivity. It's about finding a more balanced, realistic perspective.

When the Going Gets Tough: Challenges and Solutions

I'm not going to sugarcoat it: Thought replacement isn't always a walk in the park. You might face some challenges along the way. But don't worry; I've got your back with some solutions:

Challenge 1: "I can't even notice when I'm having negative thoughts!"

Solution: Start a thought journal. Set aside a few minutes each day to jot down your thoughts. This will help you become more aware of your thinking patterns.

Challenge 2: "I can identify the negative thoughts, but I struggle to challenge them."

Solution: Use the "friend test." Ask yourself, "What would I say to a friend who had this thought?" We're often much kinder to others than we are to ourselves.

Challenge 3: "I feel silly talking to myself positively."

Solution: Start small. You don't have to go from "I'm a failure" to "I'm the greatest person ever!" Small shifts toward more balanced thinking can make a big difference over time.

Challenge 4: "I try to replace the thoughts, but the negative ones keep coming back."

Solution: Remember that this is a practice. Your brain has been running its old program for a long time. Be patient and persistent. Each time you practice thought replacement, you're creating new neural pathways.

Thought replacement is a long game, and consistency is key. It's not a one-and-done kind of thing. It's more like brushing your teeth—something you need to do regularly to see the benefits. The good news is that, like any skill, it gets easier with practice. The more you practice, the more automatic the process becomes. Over time, you might find yourself naturally gravitating toward more balanced thoughts without even trying. It's like your brain develops a positivity reflex!

Key Takeaways and What's Next

This chapter has been really impactful and practical. Let's recap what we've learned:

- Thought replacement is a powerful CBT technique for combating negative thoughts.

- It's scientifically proven to be effective in improving mental health and can actually change your brain patterns over time.

- The process involves identifying negative thoughts, challenging them, and replacing them with more balanced, realistic ones.

- While you might face challenges implementing this technique, solutions like thought journaling and the "friend test" can help.

- Consistency is crucial. The more you practice, the more effective thought replacement becomes.

In the next chapter, we've got another powerful technique to learn and add to our toolbox: gratitude. Get ready to discover how a simple "thank you" can revolutionize your mental landscape.

Chapter 9:

Harnessing the Importance of Gratitude

Now, it's time to talk about the secret weapon in our fight against negative thinking. No, it's not a magic pill or a fancy gadget. It's something much simpler and more powerful: gratitude.

I know, I know; this sounds like something your great-grandmother would cross-stitch onto a pillow, but I promise there is science-backed power behind saying, "Thank you."

First, what exactly do we mean by gratitude? It's more than just saying "Thanks" when someone holds the door open for you, although that's a great start! Gratitude is a deeper appreciation for someone (or something) that produces lasting positivity.

You can think of gratitude like a mental pair of rose-colored glasses. When you put them on, you start noticing all the good stuff in your life that you might have been taking for granted. Focusing on these positive aspects can actually help kick negative thinking, stress, and anxiety to the curb.

The Science Behind Gratitude

The skeptics out there are probably crossing their arms right now and saying, "Prove it." So, let's take a look at the science again, shall we?

Studies have shown that keeping a gratitude journal can increase long-term well-being by more than ten percent (Emmons & McCullough, 2003). That's right, scribbling down a few things you're thankful for can make you happier than a ten percent pay rise! (Although, if your boss is reading this, we'll still take that raise, thanks!).

When you express gratitude, your brain releases dopamine and serotonin, two neurotransmitters that are basically responsible for making you feel good (Wright, 2023). It's like your brain has its own little pharmacy, and gratitude is the prescription.

Other studies have found that people who wrote about things they were grateful for just once a week showed significant reductions in depression levels (Komase et al., 2021). Taking just a few minutes once a week to jot down some grateful thoughts can be as effective as some forms of light therapy or sleep deprivation therapy for depression. And let's face it, writing down, "I'm grateful for pizza," is a lot more fun than staying up all night or sitting in front of a lightbox.

Benefits of Practicing Gratitude

The benefits of gratitude aren't just in your head (though there are plenty of those). Cultivating an attitude of gratitude can have some pretty impressive physical perks, too.

On the physical side, grateful people tend to

- sleep better (probably because they're not up all night worrying).

- have fewer aches and pains (it turns out that focusing on the positive is like a mental massage).

- have a stronger immune system (gratitude is like a gym membership for your white blood cells).

When it comes to mental health, the benefits are off the charts (Ackerman, 2017):

- increased happiness

- reduced depression and anxiety

- greater resilience in the face of stress

- improved self-esteem

How to Cultivate Gratitude

Now that we know that gratitude is basically a superpower, let's look at how we can start using it as one. Don't worry; you don't need to go to a gratitude gym or start mainlining thankfulness smoothies.

Here are some practical ways to start building your gratitude muscles:

The Gratitude Journal

This is Gratitude 101. Every day (or even just once a week), write down three to five things you're grateful for. They can be big things ("I'm grateful for my family's health") or small things ("I'm grateful for this really good cup of coffee"). The key is to be specific and really feel the gratitude as you write.

The Thank You Note

Channel your inner grandma and start writing thank you notes. They don't have to be for gifts. You can thank someone for being a good friend, for making you laugh, or for just being them. You get bonus points if you actually mail the note (yes, snail mail still exists).

The Gratitude Walk

Take a walk and notice all the things you're grateful for: the fresh air, the trees, the fact that your legs work and can take you on this walk. It's like a scavenger hunt for the good stuff.

The Appreciation Meditation

Spend a few minutes each day in quiet reflection, focusing on the things that you're grateful for. It's like a gratitude journal but in your head.

The Gratitude Jar

Write down one thing you're grateful for each day on a slip of paper and put it in a jar. On tough days, you can pull out a few slips of paper and remind yourself of the good stuff.

Here's a step-by-step guide to get you started:

1. Choose your gratitude practice (journal, notes, walks, etc).

2. Set a specific time each day or week for your practice.

3. Start small—aim for just one thing you're grateful for each day.

4. Be specific in your gratitude. Instead of "I'm grateful for my friend," try "I'm grateful for the way my friend always knows how to make me laugh."

5. Feel the gratitude. Don't just go through the motions—really let yourself experience the positive emotions.

6. Stick with it, even on tough days. Sometimes, finding something to be grateful for when everything seems to be going wrong is the most powerful practice of all.

As you can see, gratitude isn't just for Thanksgiving dinner or when someone buys you a gift. It's a powerful tool that can reshape your mental landscape, boost your mood, and even improve your health.

Working on an attitude of gratitude is essentially training your brain to look for the positive. And when your brain is looking for things to appreciate, it has a lot less time to dwell on the negative. It's like putting your mental space on a negativity diet and feeding it a steady stream of positivity instead.

Key Takeaways and What's Next

This chapter has taught us all about the power of gratitude. Let's recap what we've learned:

- Gratitude is a scientifically proven mood-booster and stress-buster.

- Regular gratitude practices can lead to long-term increases in happiness and well-being.

- Expressing gratitude actually changes your brain chemistry, releasing feel-good neurotransmitters.

- Gratitude has both mental and physical health benefits.

- There are many ways to practice gratitude—find the one that works best for you and make it a habit.

In the next chapter, we're going to add another tool to our positivity toolkit. We'll explore how mindfulness, affirmations, and mantras can help rewire your brain for positivity.

As we wrap up this chapter, let me just say how grateful I am for you, dear reader, for joining me on this journey to a more positive, grateful life. Now, it's time to go out there and start appreciating!

Chapter 10:

Mindfulness, Affirmations, and Mantras to Rewire Your Brain

Imagine having a remote control for your brain. Sounds pretty sci-fi, right? Well, what if I told you that you already have one? Your remote control is actually a set of powerful mental techniques that have been around for centuries, and now science is backing up their effectiveness.

You can think of this chapter as your personal guidebook to becoming the master electrician of your own mind. We're going to learn about some powerful techniques: mindfulness, affirmations, and mantras.

We'll start by identifying these practices, explore the science behind how they can literally change your brain, and then roll up our sleeves and learn how to put them into action.

Understanding Mindfulness, Affirmations, and Mantras

First things first, let's get to know our tools:

- **Mindfulness:** This is the practice of being fully present and engaged in the moment, aware of your thoughts and feelings without distraction or judgment. It's like being the observer of your own mind, watching your thoughts float by like clouds in the sky.

- **Affirmations:** These are positive statements that can help you challenge and overcome self-sabotaging and negative thoughts. Think of them as pep talks you give yourself. "I am capable and strong" is an affirmation, while "I'm such a loser" is... well, let's work on replacing that one, shall we?

- **Mantras:** These are words or sounds repeated to aid concentration in meditation. They're like affirmations' older, cooler cousin who's really into yoga. A mantra could be as simple as "Om" or as specific as "I embrace the good things in my life."

These practices aren't new. Mindfulness and mantras have their roots in ancient Eastern spiritual traditions, particularly Buddhism and Hinduism. Affirmations, while more modern, draw on similar principles of using the power of words to influence the mind.

In today's mental health landscape, these techniques have gone mainstream. Therapists often incorporate mindfulness into treatments for anxiety and depression. Affirmations are a key component of cognitive behavioral therapy. And mantras? Well, they're not just for yogis anymore. They're being used in stress reduction programs worldwide.

The Science Behind Rewiring Your Brain

Do you remember when we talked about neuroplasticity back in Chapter 1? If you remember, that's your brain's amazing ability to reorganize itself by forming new neural connections throughout life. It's like your brain is a Lego structure that can rebuild itself. And guess what? Mindfulness, affirmations, and mantras are some of the best Lego masters out there.

Hölzel et al. (2011) found that mindfulness practice led to increases in gray matter density in the hippocampus, which is known to be important for learning and memory, and in structure associated with self-awareness, compassion, and introspection. It's like mindfulness gives your brain a growth spurt.

When it comes to affirmations, Cascio et al. (2016) showed that self-affirmation activates brain systems associated with self-related processing and reward. In other words, when you affirm yourself, your brain throws a little party!

Finally, Tomasino et al. (2013) found that mantra meditation suppressed activity in the posterior cingulate cortex, an area involved in mind-wandering and self-referential thoughts. This means that mantras help your brain focus by turning down the volume on that inner chatterbox.

So, how do these practices influence neuroplasticity? They create new neural pathways and strengthen existing ones. It's like creating and reinforcing positive mental highways while letting the negative dirt roads grow over. The more you practice, the stronger these pathways become, making positive thinking more automatic over time.

Practical Steps to Incorporate These Techniques

Now that we know the "why," let's get into the "how." Here's your toolbox for rewiring your brain:

Mindfulness Practice: The Art of Being Present

1. Find a quiet, comfortable space.

2. Sit or lie down in a relaxed position.

3. Close your eyes and focus on your breath.

4. Notice the sensation of breathing without trying to change it.

5. When your mind wanders (and it will), gently bring your focus back to your breath.

6. Start with five minutes a day and gradually increase (Celestine, 2020).

Crafting Powerful Affirmations: Your Personal Pep Talk

1. Identify negative self-talk you want to change.
2. Create a positive, present-tense statement that counteracts it.
3. Make it specific and personal.
4. Keep it short and sweet.
5. Repeat your affirmation daily, ideally looking at yourself in the mirror.

Example: If you often think *I'm not good enough*, your affirmations could be, "I am worthy and capable of achieving my goals."

Mantra Magic: Focusing Your Mind

1. Choose a word, phrase, or sound that resonates with you.
2. Find a comfortable seated position.
3. Close your eyes and take a few deep breaths.
4. Begin to repeat your mantra silently or out loud.
5. If your mind wanders, gently return to your mantra.
6. Start with five to ten minutes and build up over time.

A simple mantra to start with could be: "I am at peace" or even just "peace."

Incorporating These Practices Into Your Daily Life

If you're wondering how you're supposed to start incorporating these activities into your daily life, you can consider the following:

- **Morning mindfulness:** Start your day with five minutes of mindful breathing before you get out of bed.

- **Affirmation alarm:** Set reminders on your phone to repeat your affirmations throughout the day.

- **Mantra moments:** Use waiting times (in line, at traffic lights) to silently repeat your mantra.

- **Mindful mealtime:** Practice mindful eating for one meal a day, focusing on the taste, texture, and smell of your food.

- **Bedtime affirmations:** End your day by repeating your affirmations as you lie in bed.

As you can see, these practices don't have to be an additional pressure in an already busy day. You can slot them into your usual routine without having to carve out special time. Remember, consistency is the key. These practices are like exercises for your brain, so the more regularly you do them, the stronger your mental muscles become.

Key Takeaways and What's Next

Let's recap everything we've learned in this chapter:

- Mindfulness, affirmations, and mantras are powerful tools for rewiring your brain.
    - Mindfulness is about being present and aware without judgment.
    - Affirmations are positive statements that challenge negative self-talk.
    - Mantras are repeated words or phrases that aid concentration and positive thinking.

- These practices have deep cultural roots and are now widely used in mental health treatments.

- Scientific studies show that these techniques can actually change the structure and function of your brain.

- Regular practice is crucial for creating and strengthening positive neural pathways.

- There are simple ways to incorporate these practices into your daily routine.

As you take this journey of brain renovation, please remember to be patient with yourself. Rome wasn't built in a day, and your brain won't be rewired overnight. But with consistent practice, you'll start to notice changes. You might find yourself naturally gravitating toward more positive thoughts, feeling calmer in stressful situations, or simply being more aware of the present moment.

Now that we've equipped ourselves with these powerful mental tools, it's time to put them to the test. In the next chapter, we'll learn how to use reason and evidence to challenge those pesky negative thoughts.

Chapter 11:

Challenging Negative Thoughts With Reason and Evidence

It's time to role-play. In this chapter, we're going to become Sherlock Holmes, taking part in a thrilling investigation into the case of the Sneaky Negative Thoughts. Our mission is to challenge those pesky intruders with cold, hard facts and rock-solid reasoning.

Before we dive into that, let's quickly recap our journey so far. We've unmasked the villains of negative thinking, explored the power of gratitude, and even learned how to rewire our brains. Now, we're taking it up a notch. We're not just going to observe our thoughts or replace them; we're going to challenge them head-on with the ultimate weapon: evidence.

In this chapter, we'll explore the world of cognitive distortions (fancy talk for thought traps), learn why evidence is our best ally in this battle, and arm ourselves with techniques to gather evidence. Plus, we'll hear from some fellow thought detectives who've cracked their own cases of persistent negativity.

Cognitive Distortions

So, what are cognitive distortions? Well, we discussed negative thinking traps earlier on. Simply put, they are the different ways our mind convinces us of something that isn't really true. These thought patterns often reinforce negative thinking or emotions. They are as reliable as a fake news website but far more personal.

You'll recognize some of these from earlier, but here is a more expansive list of the most common cognitive distortions. As we go through these, you might find yourself nodding along, thinking, *Hey, I do that!* Don't worry; we all do. The key is learning to recognize these thought traps so we can challenge them.

All-Or-Nothing Thinking

This is the mental equivalent of being a sore loser in a game. If you're not perfect, you're a total failure. There's no middle ground.

Example: You get a B+ on a test and think, *I'm terrible at this subject* instead of recognizing it as a good grade.

Overgeneralization

This is when you take one negative event and turn it into a never-ending pattern of defeat. It's like watching one bad movie and deciding all movies are terrible.

Example: You go on one bad date and conclude, *I'll never find love. I'm going to be alone forever.*

Mental Filter

This is like wearing gray-tinted glasses that only let you see the negative aspects of a situation. You pick out a single negative detail and dwell on it exclusively.

Example: You received praise for your presentation at work, but one person looked bored. You focus on that one person and feel like a failure.

Disqualifying the Positive

This is the fine art of turning positive experiences into negative ones. It's like having a joy-repellent shield around you.

Example: When you receive a compliment, you think, *They're just being nice*, or, *Anyone could have done that.*

Jumping to Conclusions

This comes in two flavors:

- **Mind reading:** You assume you know what people are thinking, which is usually something negative about you.

- **Fortune telling:** You predict that things will turn out badly.

Example: Your friend doesn't text back immediately, and you think, *They must be mad at me*, or *Our friendship is over*.

Magnification (Catastrophizing) or Minimizing

You blow things way out of proportion or shrink their importance inappropriately. It's like having a mental magnifying glass that you use selectively.

Example: You make a small mistake at work and think, *I'm going to get fired* (magnification), or you ace a difficult project and think, *It wasn't that big of a deal* (minimization).

Emotional Reasoning

You assume that your negative emotions reflect the way things really are: "I feel it; therefore, it must be true."

Example: *I feel like a loser, so I must be one*, or *I feel anxious, so this must be a dangerous situation*.

Should Statements

You try to motivate yourself with shoulds and should nots, as if you need to be punished before you can do anything. It's like having a drill sergeant in your head, but not the motivating kind.

Example: *I should be able to handle this*, or *I shouldn't be struggling with this task*.

Labeling

This is an extreme example of all-or-nothing thinking. Instead of saying, "I made a mistake," you label yourself, saying, "I'm a loser."

Example: After forgetting an appointment, instead of thinking, *I made a mistake*, you think, *I'm so irresponsible. I can't do anything right*.

Personalization and Blame

You see yourself as the cause of some negative external event for which you weren't primarily responsible. Alternatively, you blame others for your problems.

Example: *My son got a bad grade. I must be a terrible parent*, or *It's my boss's fault that I'm not enjoying my job*.

These distortions are incredibly common. Studies have found that even "normal" individuals engage in cognitive distortions, though to a lesser extent than those with depression (Krantz & Hammen, 1979).

Other studies have found that cognitive distortions play a significant role not just in depression but in anxiety and identity problems, too (Wang et al., 2023). It's like these distortions are the sneaky background actors in the drama of our mental health, influencing the plot without us even realizing it.

The good news is that once you start recognizing these distortions in your thinking, you've already taken the first step toward challenging them. It's like shining a spotlight on the magician's tricks—once you see how it's done, the illusion loses its power.

Next, let's explore why evidence is our best weapon against these tricky thought patterns and how we can use it to our advantage.

The Role of Evidence in Challenging Negative Thoughts

So, why is evidence so effective in challenging these cognitive distortions? Well, it's all about bringing our thoughts back down to Earth, grounding them in reality rather than letting them float off into the stratosphere of negativity.

Our brains are naturally biased toward negative information. It's an evolutionary hangover from when being alert to dangers was crucial for survival. Studies have found that this negativity bias can significantly impact our information processing and decision-making (Molins et al., 2022).

To make matters more complicated, we also have to contend with confirmation bias—our brain's tendency to search for, interpret, and recall information in a way that confirms our preexisting beliefs. When it comes to negative thinking, this means we're more likely to notice and remember information that supports our negative beliefs while ignoring or discounting positive information.

Mathews and MacLeod (2005) provided strong evidence for this bias, particularly in individuals with anxiety disorders. They found that anxious individuals were more likely to interpret ambiguous information in a threatening way. For instance, if an anxious person hears laughter when they walk into a room, they're more likely to assume people are laughing at them rather than considering other possibilities.

More recent research has shown this bias isn't limited to anxiety. Everaert et al. (2017) found that individuals with depression were more likely to interpret ambiguous scenarios negatively, and this negative interpretation bias predicted more severe depressive symptoms over time.

So, with our brains seemingly working against us, how do we break free from this negativity trap? This is where evidence comes in, and here's why it's so powerful:

- **Evidence grounds thoughts in reality:** When we gather evidence, we bring ourselves back to reality instead of letting our thoughts run away with crazy ideas.

- **Evidence challenges our biases:** By actively seeking out and considering all information—not just the stuff that confirms our negative beliefs—we can start to break free from confirmation bias.

- **Our brains respond to facts:** While our brains might be predisposed to focus on the negative, they're also wired to respond to facts. When we consciously gather and present evidence to our minds, we're essentially fact-checking our own thoughts.

- **Evidence provides a balanced perspective:** By considering both supporting and contradictory evidence, we can develop a more balanced, realistic view of situations and ourselves.

- **Gathering evidence is an active process:** Unlike rumination, which is passive and often unproductive, gathering evidence requires us to engage actively with our thoughts. This shift in approach can be beneficial.

Using evidence to challenge our thoughts is like turning on the lights in a dark room. Suddenly, we can see things more clearly, including the positive aspects we might have missed.

Techniques for Gathering Evidence Against Negative Thoughts

Now that we know why evidence is so powerful, let's equip ourselves with some techniques to gather it. Here are three powerful tools for your mental detective kit:

The Thought Record

This is like keeping a logbook of your mental investigations. Here's how to do it:

1. Write down the situation that triggered the negative thought.

2. Note the automatic thought that popped into your head.

3. Rate how much you believe this thought (0–100).

4. List the evidence that doesn't support the thought.

5. Come up with a more balanced thought based on all the evidence.

6. Re-rate how much you believe the original thought (*How To Use CBT Thought Records To Change The Way You Feel*, n.d.).

The Behavioral Experiment

This is where you put your thoughts to the test in the real world. Here's the process:

1. Identify a negative prediction (e.g., "If I speak up in the meeting, everyone will think I'm stupid.").

2. Rate how much you believe this (0–100).

3. Design an experiment to test this prediction (e.g., speak up in the next meeting and observe reactions).

4. Carry out the experiment and record what actually happened.

5. Compare the results to your prediction and re-rate your belief.

The Survey Method

This involves gathering evidence from others. Here's how:

1. Identify a negative belief about yourself (e.g., "I'm too boring to talk to.").

2. Create a short, neutral question to ask others (e.g., "How would you describe me in social situations?").

3. Ask a variety of people and record their responses.

4. Compare their feedback to your belief.

The key to all of these techniques is to approach them with genuine curiosity. You're not trying to prove yourself wrong; you're simply investigating to find out what's really true.

Case Studies

Let's look at how some real people have put these techniques into action:

Case Study 1: Casey's Social Anxiety

Casey was convinced that she was socially awkward and that people didn't enjoy talking to her. Using the survey method, she asked ten friends and colleagues how they perceived her in social situations. To her surprise, most described her as "thoughtful," "good listener," and "interesting to talk to." This evidence directly contradicted her negative beliefs and helped her feel more confident in social situations.

Case Study 2: Kiera's Work Worries

Kiera constantly worried that her work wasn't good enough and that she was on the verge of being fired. She used the thought record technique to challenge these beliefs. By writing down evidence for and against her thoughts, she realized that she had consistently received positive feedback from her boss and had even been given more responsibilities recently. This helped her see that her fears were not based on reality.

Key Takeaways and What's Next

As we close up this chapter, remember that challenging your thoughts with evidence isn't about proving yourself wrong or right. It's about seeing the full picture, not just the negative snapshot your mind sometimes presents.

If you practice these techniques, you'll be training your brain to be a more objective observer of your experiences. Over time, you'll likely find that your first response to negative thoughts isn't blind acceptance but a curious "Is that really true? Let's investigate!"

Here's what we learned in this chapter:

- Cognitive distortions are common thought traps that can fuel negative thinking.

- Our brains have a natural negativity bias, but they also respond to facts and evidence.

- Techniques like thought records, behavioral experiments, and the survey method can help us gather evidence to challenge negative thoughts.

- Approaching these techniques with genuine curiosity is key to their effectiveness.

- Real people have successfully used these methods to overcome persistent negative thinking.

- The goal is not to always think positively but to think more accurately and see the full picture.

Now that we've learned how to challenge our negative thoughts, it's time to take it a step further. In the next chapter, we'll explore the art of reframing—turning those negative thoughts into positive ones.

Chapter 12:

Turning Negatives Into Positives—the Art of Reframing, Visualization and the "Yes, But" Trick

Now, we're going to learn some advanced techniques in the art of positive thinking. This chapter is going to dive into the world of reframing, visualization, and a nifty little trick I like to call the "Yes, but" technique. Let's add to your toolkit for transforming those pesky negative thoughts into shiny, positive ones.

Understanding Reframing

First, we have reframing. Just so you know, we're not talking about actual picture frames here. We're talking about the mental frames we put around our experiences and thoughts.

Reframing is a cognitive-behavioral technique that involves identifying negative or unhelpful thoughts and then changing the "frame" around them to view the situation in a more positive or productive light. It's like taking a gloomy landscape and putting in a brighter, more cheerful frame—suddenly, it doesn't look so bad after all.

This isn't a new idea, either. Back in 1988, Meichenbaum and Deffenbacher studied something called stress inoculation training, which includes cognitive restructuring or reframing. They found that this technique was effective in helping people manage stress and anxiety (Meichenbaum & Deffenbacher, 1988).

However, before we can reframe our thoughts, we need to become expert thought-catchers. This is where the work of Dr. Aaron Beck comes in. Beck, often called the father of cognitive therapy, identified common cognitive distortions that lead to negative thinking (Whalley,

2019). These include things like all-or-nothing thinking, overgeneralization, and catastrophizing. (Sound familiar? We talked about these in earlier chapters!).

Steps for Reframing Negative Thoughts

Now, let's learn how to flip the script on these thoughts. In his book *Feeling Good: The New Mood Therapy*, David Burns (1999) builds on Beck's cognitive therapy. He shows that by systematically identifying, challenging, and reframing negative thoughts, we can significantly reduce symptoms of depression and anxiety. In fact, studies have shown that these cognitive techniques can be as effective as medication for many people suffering from mood disorders (APA, 2017).

So, how do we actually do this reframing thing? Here's a step-by-step guide:

1. **Acknowledge the thought:** This is where your thought-catching skills come in handy. Burns emphasizes the importance of becoming aware of our "automatic thoughts"—those quick, evaluative thoughts that pop into our heads throughout the day. Example: *I made a mistake on that report. I'm so stupid.*

2. **Challenge it:** Burns calls this step "evaluating the automatic thought." Here, we play devil's advocate with our own thoughts. We look for evidence that contradicts our negative beliefs and questions the logic behind it. Ask yourself:

    A. Is this thought based on facts or feelings?

    B. Am I jumping to conclusions?

    C. Am I holding myself to an unreasonable standard? Example: *Is making one mistake really evidence of stupidity? Haven't I done many things well in the past?*

3. **Replace it:** This is what Burns refers to as "rational response." Here, we create a new thought that is more balanced and realistic. Example: *Everyone makes mistakes sometimes. This doesn't reflect my intelligence. I can learn from this and do better next time.*

Research shows that consistently practicing these steps leads to significant improvements in mood and reductions in negative thinking (Burns, 1999). In one study, patients who learned these cognitive techniques showed as much improvement as those treated with antidepressant medication.

The key, again, was consistency. Burns found that those who practiced these techniques regularly—even for just a few minutes each day—saw the most significant improvements.

Here's a quick exercise to help you practice:

1. Write down a negative thought you've had recently.

2. Use the three steps above to reframe it.

3. Notice how you feel after reframing. Any difference?

You don't have to force yourself to think positively all the time. As Burns points out, the aim is to think more realistically and balanced. Sometimes, things really are difficult or disappointing.

What Is Visualization and How Can It Help Reframe Thoughts?

Now, let's consider visualization. This technique involves creating a mental image of what you want to happen or how you want to feel. It's like being a director of your own mental movie.

Why is visualization so powerful? Studies have found that people who visualized themselves practicing a piano exercise showed almost the same level of improvement as those who actually practiced physically

(Frank et al., 2014). It's like your brain can't quite tell the difference between imagination and reality.

It's not just for physical skills. Renner et al. (2019) found that positive mental imagery can significantly improve mood and reduce anxiety. You can give your brain a happy little vacation, even if your body is stuck at your desk.

Types of Visualization Exercises for Positive Thinking and How to Use It

So, how can we use visualization to reframe our thoughts? Here are a few techniques:

Guided Imagery

This involves imagining a peaceful, safe place when you're feeling stressed or anxious. Close your eyes and picture yourself on a beautiful beach or in a serene forest. Engage all your senses. What do you see, hear, smell, or feel?

Vision Boarding

Create a collage of images that represent your goals and positive affirmations. Place it somewhere you'll see often. It's like creating a movie poster for your ideal life.

Mental Rehearsal

Before a challenging situation, visualize yourself handling it successfully. Imagine yourself giving that presentation with confidence or acing that job interview.

Here's a quick visualization exercise to try:

1. Close your eyes and take a few deep breaths.

2. Think of a recent negative thought you've had.

3. Now, imagine that thought as a dark cloud.

4. Visualize a gentle breeze coming along and blowing that cloud away, replacing it with bright sunshine.

5. Feel the warmth of that sunshine and the positivity it brings.

Practice this whenever you catch yourself in a negative thought spiral. Your brain is pretty gullible, so make sure you feed it positive images, and it'll start to believe them.

Understanding the "Yes, But" Technique

Last but not least, let's talk about the "Yes, but" technique. This is a great little trick that can help you challenge negative thoughts on the spot.

Here's how it works: When you catch yourself in a negative thought, acknowledge it (that's the "Yes" part), but then immediately follow it with a positive or more balanced statement (that's the "But" part).

For example:

- Negative thought: *I made a mistake on that report. I'm so stupid.*

- "Yes, but" reframe: *Yes, I made a mistake, but mistakes are how we learn and improve.*

Studies have found that thought replacement techniques like this can effectively reduce pathological worry in people with generalized anxiety disorder (Eagleson et al., 2016).

To make this a habit, try these steps:

1. Catch the negative thought.
2. Say "Yes" to acknowledge it.
3. Add a "But" followed by a more positive or balanced statement.
4. Practice, practice, practice.

Here's an exercise to get you started: For the next week, every time you have a negative thought, try the "Yes, but" technique. Keep a tally of how many times you use it. You might be surprised at how often you have the opportunity to practice.

Key Takeaways and What's Next

Mastering these techniques takes time and practice, as with everything we've learned so far throughout this book.

Let's recap what we've learned in this chapter:

- Reframing involves acknowledging, challenging, and replacing negative thoughts.
- Visualization can be as effective as physical practice in some cases.
- The "Yes, but" technique helps balance negative thoughts with positive ones.
- Consistent practice is key to making these techniques effective.

Now, I think we're ready to tackle negativity in specific areas of our lives. In the next chapter, we'll explore how to apply these techniques to common problem areas like work stress, relationship issues, and self-image concerns.

Chapter 13:

Overcoming Negativity in Key Life Areas

We've spent our time so far gathering all our resources and getting ready to combat negative thinking. Now, it's time to apply these skills to battlegrounds where negativity loves to wage war: our work lives, our relationships, our body image, and our finances.

Silencing Your Inner Critic at Work and Dealing With Others

Let's start with the voice in your head that's been holding your career hostage. You know the one I'm talking about—that nagging inner critic that tells you you're not good enough, smart enough, or qualified enough. It's like having a really mean boss living rent-free in your brain, and it's time to serve that boss an eviction notice!

Understanding Your Inner Critic

Let's start by getting to know this unwelcome guest. Your inner critic is that part of your psyche that's constantly judging and evaluating you. It's like having a perpetual performance review but with a really unfair and biased reviewer.

This critic can manifest in various ways:

- "I'm going to mess up this presentation."

- "Everyone else is more qualified than me."

- "I don't deserve this promotion."

- "They're going to find out I'm a fraud."

Sound familiar? You're not alone. In fact, there's a whole body of research on this pesky critic. Researchers have found that self-criticism is linked to a whole host of mental health issues, including depression, anxiety, and even eating disorders (Montero-Marín et al., 2016).

This self-criticism isn't just making you feel bad; it's actually sabotaging your work performance. It's like trying to run a marathon with a ball and chain attached to your ankle. You might still finish, but it's going to be a lot harder and less enjoyable than it needs to be.

Impact of Negative Self-Talk at Work

Now, let's talk about how this negative self-talk is messing with your 9-to-5 (or 8-to-late for some of us). This constant stream of self-doubt and criticism can:

- **Tank your performance:** When you're constantly second-guessing yourself, you're less likely to take risks or propose innovative ideas. It's like having a creativity vampire sucking all the good ideas out of your brain.

- **Zap your productivity:** Have you ever spent hours agonizing over an email because you're worried about how it will be received? That's your inner critic stealing your time and energy.

- **Strain your work relationships:** If you're constantly down on yourself, it can affect how you interact with colleagues. You might come across as defensive, withdrawn, or overly self-deprecating.

- **Block your career growth:** Why apply for that promotion if you're "not good enough anyway," right? Wrong! Your inner critic might be holding you back from amazing opportunities.

- **Increase your stress levels:** Constant self-criticism is like having a stress faucet that's always on. And we all know that chronic stress is about as good for you as a daily diet of donuts and energy drinks.

Silencing Your Inner Critic

Now, let's talk about solutions. Let's learn how to silence that inner critic and let your inner cheerleader take the mic. Cognitive behavioral therapy has been found to be incredibly effective in treating anxiety disorders (Hoffman & Smits, 2008; Hofmann et al., 2012). If it can tackle clinical anxiety, it can definitely help with your workplace worries.

Here are some strategies based on CBT that can help:

- **Catch and challenge:** When you notice a negative thought, stop and challenge it. Is there actual evidence for this thought? Or is your inner critic just making stuff up?

- **Reframe:** Turn those negative thoughts into more balanced, positive ones. Instead of, *I'm going to mess up this presentation*, try *This is an opportunity to share my ideas and learn from the experience.*

- **Create a success file:** Keep a record of your achievements, positive feedback, and wins (big and small). Next time your inner critic pipes up, whip out this file for a reality check. It's like having a highlight reel of your career that is always ready to play.

- **Use the "yet" trick:** When your inner critic says, "I'm not good at public speaking," add a "yet" to the end. "I'm not good at public speaking... yet." It's amazing how one little word can shift your perspective from a fixed to a growth mindset.

Dealing with Criticism From Others

Of course, sometimes the criticism actually does come from outside your own head. Here are some tips for how to handle it without letting it fuel your inner critic:

- **Separate the wheat from the chaff:** Ask yourself if this criticism is constructive. If it is, consider how you can use it to improve. If not, practice letting go. Not all opinions need to be taken to heart.

- **Respond, don't react:** Take a breath before responding to criticism. This gives you time to process and respond thoughtfully rather than defensively. It's like having a mental pause button.

- **Use the feedback sandwich:** When giving criticism to others, sandwich it between two positive comments. This technique can also help you reframe the criticism you receive. "Okay, they said my teamwork was great, but I need to improve my time management. They also praised my creativity."

- **Ask for specifics:** If someone's criticism is vague, ask for concrete examples. This can help you address real issues and also call out criticism that's not based on facts.

- **Remember that criticism isn't always about you:** Sometimes, a person's criticism says more about them than it does about you. Maybe your boss is having a bad day, or your colleague is feeling insecure. Don't automatically internalize others' negativity.

Building Resilience and Maintaining Positivity

Resilience is your secret weapon in the workplace. It's like having a force field that helps negative experiences bounce off you. Here's how you can build your resilience muscles:

- **Use positive affirmations:** Start your workday with positive affirmations. "I am capable and confident in my abilities" can set a powerful tone for the day. It's like being your own personal hype person.

- **Celebrate small wins:** Acknowledge your daily achievements, no matter how small. Finished a report? Give yourself a mental high five! It's about progress, not perfection.

- **Build a support network:** Surround yourself with positive, supportive colleagues. Having a work bestie can make even the toughest day more bearable.

- **Practice gratitude:** Take a moment each day to appreciate something about your job, no matter how small. Maybe it's your comfy office chair or the way Karen always remembers how you like your coffee.

- **Take care of your physical health:** Exercise, eat well, and get enough sleep. A healthy body supports a resilient mind. It's hard to be emotionally strong when you're running on empty and on a diet of vending machine snacks.

As with everything we've learned so far, resilience also takes time and consistency to build. Over time, you'll find yourself bouncing back from setbacks faster and maintaining a more positive outlook, even when work gets tough.

Impact of Negative Thinking on Relationships

Now, let's consider relationships. Negative thinking is the ultimate party pooper in any relationship. Let's learn how this negativity can turn your love story into a horror flick and, more importantly, how to rewrite the script for a happier ending.

How Bad Thoughts Infect Good Relationships

You're in a relationship with someone great. They're kind and funny, and they always remember to pick up your favorite ice cream. But for some reason, you can't shake the feeling that something's off. You find yourself nitpicking, arguing over small things, and generally feeling unsatisfied. Congratulations! You might have caught the negativity virus.

Constant negativity can lead to a trifecta of relationship doom: conflict, misunderstanding, and resentment (Dean, 2024). It's like inviting a third wheel on all your dates, but instead of just being awkward, this third wheel is actively trying to sabotage your relationships.

Here's how negativity messes with your love life:

- **Conflict creation:** When you're stuck in a negative mindset, you're more likely to interpret your partner's actions in a negative light. Did they forget to text you back? Clearly, they don't care about you (spoiler alert: they probably just got busy at work).

- **Misunderstanding mania:** Negative thinking can make you jump to conclusions faster than an Olympic long jumper. This leads to misunderstandings that could have been avoided with a simple conversation.

- **Resentment buildup:** Over time, all these negative interpretations and misunderstandings can lead to resentment.

- **Perception distortion:** Negativity doesn't just affect how you interact with your partner; it changes how you see the entire relationship. You might start focusing only on the bad parts, forgetting all the good stuff that made you fall in love in the first place.

- **Self-fulfilling prophecy:** If you constantly think your relationship is doomed, guess what? You might just make it come true. It's like manifesting but for pessimists.

Signs of Persistent Negativity in Relationships

So, how do you know if negativity has overstayed its welcome in your relationship? Here are some signs to watch out for:

- **Argument avalanche:** You find yourselves bickering more often than not, even over small things like whose turn it is to do the dishes.

- **Communication breakdown:** You're talking but not really communicating. It's like you're speaking different languages, and neither of you bothered to bring a translator.

- **Emotional drain:** After spending time together, you feel exhausted rather than energized.

- **Criticism central:** You or your partner have become a constant critic, always pointing out what's wrong instead of what's right.

- **Defensive stance:** You're both always on guard, ready to defend yourselves at the slightest provocation. It's like you're in a verbal boxing match, but nobody ever wins.

- **Negative nostalgia:** When you think about your relationship, you focus more on past hurts than happy memories.

- **Lack of intimacy:** I'm not just talking about physical intimacy here. There's an emotional distance that feels like a Grand Canyon between you.

Before you panic or call your lawyer, remember that all relationships have their ups and downs. It's normal to go through rough patches. The key is to differentiate between normal relationship hiccups and persistent negative patterns.

If you're experiencing one or two of these signs occasionally, it's probably just a normal relationship speed bump. But if you're nodding along to most of these and thinking, *Yes, that's us most of the time*, then Houston, we might have a problem to work on.

Techniques to Reduce and Eliminate Negativity From Your Relationships

All hope is not lost! Even if negativity has taken up residence in your relationship, there are ways to evict it. Let's look at some techniques backed by science—because who doesn't love a little research with their relationship advice?

- **Thought stopping:** When you catch yourself in a negative thought spiral about your partner, imagine a big red STOP sign. Give yourself a mental traffic light for your negative thoughts.

- **Cognitive restructuring:** Challenge those negative thoughts. Is *My partner never listens to me* really true, or is it more accurate to think *Sometimes, I don't feel heard*? It's about finding a more balanced perspective.

- **Positive focus:** Make a conscious effort to notice and appreciate your partner's positive qualities and actions. It's like being a detective, but instead of looking for clues to solve a crime, you're looking for reasons to appreciate your partner.

- **The benefit of the doubt:** When your partner does something that annoys you, try assuming a positive intent. Maybe they're not trying to annoy you; maybe they're just human and make mistakes sometimes.

- **Mindfulness in communication:** Pay attention to how you're communicating. Are you expressing your needs clearly, or are you expecting your partner to be a mind reader? (Epstein & Baucom, 2002).

Cultivating Positivity in Your Relationships

Now that we've tackled the negativity, let's focus on boosting the positivity in your relationship. Research into psychological interventions in close relationships has shown that some strategies really can make a difference (Proulx et al., 2018):

- **Gratitude galore:** Regularly express appreciation for your partner. "Thank you for making dinner" goes a long way, leaving little deposits in your relationship's emotional bank account.

- **Shared positive experiences:** Plan activities you both enjoy. Whether it's hiking, cooking, or binge-watching your favorite show, shared joy is double joy!

- **Strength spotting:** Focus on each other's strengths. Instead of harping on weaknesses, celebrate what your partner is good at.

- **Acts of kindness:** Do something nice for your partner without expecting anything in return. It could be as simple as bringing them their favorite coffee or giving them a spontaneous hug.

- **Open communication:** Create a safe space to discuss feelings and concerns. Remember, it's you and your partner versus the problem, not versus each other.

- **Positive reminiscence:** Regularly revisit happy memories together.

- **Future dreaming:** Talk about your hopes and dreams for the future. It's not just practical planning; it's a way of saying, "I see a future with you, and I'm excited about it!"

Your Turn: A Quick Negativity Check-In

Now, it's time to put all this knowledge into action. Here's a quick exercise to help you identify any negativity in your relationship and start turning things around:

1. Take a moment to reflect on your relationship over the past week.

2. Write down any instances where you noticed negativity (in your thoughts, words, or actions).

3. For each negative instance, try to reframe it in a more positive or balanced way.

4. Now, write down three things you appreciate about your partner.

5. Commit to sharing at least one of these appreciations with your partner today.

Each positive thought, word, and action will help you build a stronger, happier relationship over time.

Conquering Negative Thinking about Your Body, Appearance and Aging

Negative body image is something that has been haunting many of us since puberty hit. It's that little voice that pops up every time you look in the mirror or try on clothes or, heaven forbid, see a photo of yourself on social media. Well, it's time to tell that voice to pipe down! Let's start working on body positivity and self-love.

Understanding Negative Body Image

Let's start by defining what we're dealing with here: Negative body image is when you have a distorted, negative view of your body that doesn't match reality.

This is not a rare condition. In our society, negative body image is about as common as selfies on Instagram. We're bombarded with images of "perfect" bodies faster than you can say "Photoshop." Magazines, TV, movies, and especially social media are constantly showing us idealized, often unrealistic, body types. We're all contestants in a beauty pageant that we never signed up for, and the judges are particularly harsh.

Connection Between Negative Body Image and Mental Health

Negative body image can have serious consequences for your mental health. Strong links have been found between negative body image and a whole host of mental health issues (Quittkat et al., 2019). We're talking about anxiety, depression, and eating disorders.

Here's how it typically goes down:

1. You have negative thoughts about your body.

2. These thoughts make you feel bad about yourself.

3. Feeling bad about yourself leads to anxiety or depression.

4. Anxiety or depression might lead to unhealthy behaviors (like distorted eating).

5. These behaviors reinforce the negative body image.

6. And round and round we go on the not-so-merry-go-round of negativity.

Impact of Societal Standards on Self-Perception

Unfortunately, society has impossible standards that completely mess with our heads. These unrealistic standards are like a bad recipe:

1. Take one part impossibly thin body.

2. Add a dash of eternal youth.

3. Mix in some flawless skin.

4. Sprinkle with whatever feature is trending on social media this week.

5. Bake under the heat of constant societal pressure.

6. Serve with a side of "Why don't I look like that?"

Social media is another can of worms. It's like a highlight reel of everyone's best angles, perfect lighting, and expertly applied filters. It's no wonder we feel like we don't measure up!

Accepting Aging as a Natural Process

Many of us fear aging like it's the bogeyman of adulthood, but it really doesn't have to be that way. It's actually the only alternative to dying young, so let's learn how to embrace the silver fox or vixen within, shall we?

Common fears about aging include:

- loss of attractiveness (as if beauty has an expiration date!)
- decreased vitality (tell that to the 80-year-olds running marathons)
- becoming irrelevant (because apparently, wisdom counts for nothing?)

Aging is a natural, beautiful process. In their research, Zanjari et al. (2017) discuss the concept of aging gracefully. It's about embracing the changes, celebrating the wisdom you've gained, and continuing to grow and thrive.

Don't think of aging as getting older; think of it like leveling up. Each year brings new experiences, new knowledge, and, yes, maybe a few new wrinkles. But those wrinkles are like your life's road map, showing all the places you've been and the things you've seen.

Fostering Positive Attitudes Toward One's Body

Let's take a look at some tips to help you cultivate body positivity and self-love:

- **Focus on function over form:** Celebrate what your body can do instead of obsessing over how it looks.
- **Curate your social media:** If there are any accounts that make you feel bad about yourself, unfollow them. Be sure to only follow body-positive accounts that celebrate diversity.
- **Wear clothes that make you feel good:** Don't wait to lose weight or change your body to wear clothes you love. Dress your current body with love and respect.

- **Practice self-care:** Treat your body like you would a beloved friend. Nourish it, rest it, and move it in ways that feel good.

- **Compliment others genuinely:** Spreading positivity can also help you feel more positive. But remember to compliment people on more than just their appearance!

- **Focus on health, not size:** Health comes in many shapes and sizes. Focus on behaviors that make you feel good and energized.

- **Speak to yourself kindly:** If you wouldn't say it to your best friend, don't say it to yourself.

- **Use positive affirmations:** These are like push-ups for your self-esteem. Try these on for size:
    - "I am more than my appearance."
    - "My body is a gift, and I treat it with respect."
    - "I choose to feel comfortable in my own skin."

- **Practice yoga:** This is not just for Instagram influencers. Yoga can help you connect with your body in a positive way. Plus, it's a great reminder that your body is capable of amazing things.

You are so much more than your appearance. You're a complex, fascinating, valuable human being with thoughts, feelings, talents, and experiences that make you uniquely you. Your body is the vessel that carries all of that amazingness around, and for that alone, it deserves your love and respect.

Next time you look in the mirror, try to see what your loved ones see when they look at you: a beautiful, worthy person who deserves all the love in the world—starting with your own!

Releasing Negativity Surrounding Money and Finances

It's time to talk about everyone's favorite topic: money. Or maybe it's your least favorite topic. Either way, we're diving in, so hold onto your wallet!

For many of us, thinking about money is about as enjoyable as a root canal. However, your thoughts about money could be affecting your bank account more than you realize. So let's break down those money mental blocks and start building a fortune... or at least stop hiding from our credit card bills.

Understanding Negative Thinking About Money

Let's begin by talking about how your thoughts about money can impact your financial decisions. And no, I'm not talking about manifesting millions by thinking positive thoughts (though if that works for you, more power to you!).

A study by Vohs, Mead, and Goode (2006) dramatically titled *The Psychological Consequences of Money* (sounds like a great horror movie, doesn't it?) found that even just thinking about money can change our behavior. And not always for the better.

Here are some common negative thought patterns about money:

- **Scarcity mindset:** *There's never enough money.* This is like thinking you're always on a financial diet.

- **Money guilt:** *I don't deserve to have money.* Reality check: Yes, you do!

- **Fear of debt:** *All debt is bad.* While credit card debt from your last shopping spree might not be great, some debt (like a mortgage) can be a tool for building wealth.

- **Money avoidance:** *If I don't look at my bank account, my problems will go away.* Reality check #2: No, they won't.

- **Magical thinking:** *I'll start saving when I make more money.* Future you is rolling their eyes right now.

These thought patterns can lead to poor financial decisions faster than you can say "impulse purchase." They might cause you to overspend, under-save, or avoid dealing with your finances altogether. Your negative thoughts are the high-interest credit card of your mind!

Identifying and Challenging Your Negative Thoughts About Money

Time for some financial self-reflection. Grab a pen and paper (or your Notes app, if you prefer) because we're about to do some thought-catching.

Common negative beliefs about money include:

- *Money is the root of all evil.*
- *Rich people are greedy.*
- *I'll never be good with money.*
- *I don't make enough to save.*
- *Talking about money is taboo.*

Do any of these sound familiar? Write down any negative money thoughts you have. Go on, I'll wait. Got them? Great! Now, let's challenge these thoughts using some cognitive behavioral techniques.

- **Evidence checking:** For each negative belief, ask yourself: "Is this really true? What evidence do I have for and against this belief?"

- **Reframing:** Turn that negative thought into a more balanced or positive one. "I'll never be good with money" becomes "I'm learning to manage my money better every day."

- **Positive affirmations:** Create positive statements about money. "I am capable of making smart financial decisions." Repeat these daily. It might feel silly at first, but stick with it!

Lally and Gardner's (2013) study on habit formation suggests it takes an average of 66 days to form a new habit. So, don't expect your money mindset to change overnight. It's a marathon, not a sprint (much like saving for retirement, am I right?).

Here are some practical exercises to help shift your money mindset:

- **Gratitude journaling:** Each day, write down three things you're grateful for financially. Maybe you're thankful for your job or that you were able to pay a bill on time.

- **Visualization:** Imagine your ideal financial future. What does it look like? How does it feel? The more vivid, the better.

- **Money diary:** For a week, write down every purchase you make and how it makes you feel. This can help you identify emotional spending triggers.

Setting Financial Goals and Planning For the Future

Now that we're shifting that money mindset, let's talk about setting some financial goals. By the way, "being rich" is not a goal. It's a daydream—we need specifics!

Setting realistic financial goals is crucial. It's like planning a road trip: You need to know where you are going and how you're going to get there. Here's how to get started:

- **Be SMART:** Make your goals specific, measurable, achievable, relevant, and time-bound. "I want to save $5,000 for a down payment on a car in 18 months" is a SMART goal.

- **Short-term vs. long-term:** Have a mix of both. Short-term could be building an emergency fund, while long-term might be saving for retirement.

- **Write them down:** There's power in putting pen to paper (or fingers to keyboard). Write down your goals and put them somewhere you'll see often.

Now let's talk about some practical tools to help you reach these goals:

- **Budgeting:** I know, I know, it's not sexy. But neither is being broke. Track your income and expenses. There are plenty of apps that can help make this less painful.

- **The debt snowball:** This is financial guru Dave Ramsey's idea (Kamel, 2023). Pay minimum payments on all debts, but throw any extra money at your smallest debt. When that's paid off, move to the next smallest and lump the extra cash into this payment. It's satisfying and motivating.

- **Pay yourself first:** Treat savings like a bill. Set up automatic transfers to your savings account each payday.

- **Educate yourself:** Learn about investing. You don't need to become a Wall Street wizard, but understanding basics like compounding interest can be a game-changer.

- **Celebrate wins:** Did you stick to your budget this month? Treat yourself (within reason, of course)! Positive reinforcement works wonders.

Your relationship with money is just that—a relationship. It requires attention, care, and sometimes, a bit of couples counseling (you and your wallet are the couple in this scenario, just to be clear). But with time and effort, you can turn your financial frowns upside down and start building the wealth you deserve.

Key Takeaways and What's Next

This has been quite an intense chapter! We've covered a lot, from the boardroom to the bedroom to the mirror to the wallet. Overcoming negativity in these key areas of life is a journey, not a destination. So, be patient with yourself and celebrate your progress along the way.

Let's recap:

- Silence your inner work critic with CBT techniques and build resilience.

- Nurture positive relationships by challenging negative thoughts and practicing gratitude.

- Combat negative body image by questioning societal standards and practicing body appreciation.

- Transform your relationship with money by identifying negative beliefs and setting positive financial goals.

Up next, we're going to start thinking about the long game. In the next chapter, we'll explore how to maintain a positive mindset for the long haul, including lifestyle changes that support positive thinking.

PART 4: Maintaining a Positive Mindset Long-Term

Chapter 14:

Lifestyle Changes to Support Positive Thinking

Welcome to the final part of this book. So far, we've gathered different tools to help you combat negative thinking. Now, we're going to give your whole lifestyle a positivity makeover. We're going to learn how to create a life that naturally supports positive thinking. We're talking diet, exercise, sleep, and even interior design (yes, really!).

The Surprising Link Between Diet, Exercise, and Negative Thoughts

Let's start by discussing two things that might seem completely unrelated to your thoughts: what's on your plate and how much you're moving that beautiful body of yours. This is not going to be another lecture about eating your veggies and hitting the gym. Hear me out. This is not about fitting into your skinny jeans or getting abs of steel. It's about feeding your brain the good stuff and giving it the movement it craves to keep those positive vibes flowing.

The Gut-Brain Connection

It turns out that your gut and your brain are actually besties. They're constantly chatting, and what you eat can seriously impact your mood. Studies have found that people who eat a lot of processed foods and sugar are more likely to be depressed (Lassale et al., 2019). It's a bit like feeding your brain a steady diet of sad movies and breakup songs. On the flip side, those who munched on more fruits, vegetables, and fish were less likely to be depressed.

Why does this happen? Well, certain foods can affect your brain function more directly than you might think. Take sugar, for example.

Sure, it gives you a quick energy boost, but it's followed by a crash that can leave you feeling irritable and moody.

Serotonin: The Happiness Hormone

Your body produces this chemical to help regulate mood, and guess what? Certain foods can help boost its production. It's like having a happiness factory in your body, and the right foods are the workers that keep it running smoothly.

Foods that can boost serotonin production include (Mandriota, 2022; Sissons, 2024):

- bananas
- eggs
- cheese
- turkey
- nuts and seeds
- salmon and other fatty fish

These foods are like nature's own antidepressants, and the best part is that there's no prescription required!

How a Healthy Diet Can Help Reduce Negative Thoughts

Now that we know certain foods can boost our mood, let's talk about how a balanced diet can help keep those negative thoughts at bay.

- **Stable blood sugar = stable mood:** When your blood sugar is on a roller coaster, your mood goes along for the ride. Eating balanced meals with complex carbs, protein, and healthy fats can help keep your blood sugar (and mood) stable.

- **Nutrient-rich foods = brain fuel:** Your brain needs certain nutrients to function optimally. Omega-3 fatty acids, B vitamins, and antioxidants are like premium gasoline for your brain.

- **Gut health = mental health:** Remember that gut-brain connection we talked about? Eating foods rich in probiotics (like yogurt or kimchi) can help keep your gut healthy, which in turn can improve your mood.

- **Hydration = clear thinking:** Even mild dehydration can affect your mood and cognitive function. So drink up! Water, that is.

Practical Tips for Eating Your Way to Positivity

1. Start your day with a protein-rich breakfast. It'll stabilize your blood sugar and mood. Think eggs with whole-grain toast or Greek yogurt with berries and nuts.

2. Snack on nuts and seeds for a serotonin boost. A handful of almonds or pumpkin seeds can be your afternoon pick-me-up.

3. Include fatty fish in your diet for those omega-3s. Aim for at least two servings a week. Not a fan of fish? You can try chia seeds or flaxseeds.

4. Don't skip meals. Hangry is not a positive emotion! Keep healthy snacks on hand for busy days.

5. Limit processed foods and sugar. Your brain will thank you. When you do indulge (because, let's face it, sometimes you need that cookie), pair it with some protein to minimize the blood sugar spike.

6. Eat the rainbow. Different colored fruits and vegetables offer different nutrients. Plus, a colorful plate is just more fun to eat!

Exercise as a Tool Against Stress and Anxiety

Now, let's talk about the E-word: exercise. Before you close this book and run for the hills (which, incidentally, would be great exercise), hear me out. I am not about to tell you to become a gym rat or run marathons. We're going to talk about moving your body in ways that feel good and give your brain a happiness boost.

When you exercise, your body releases chemicals called endorphins. These little guys are like nature's antidepressants. They reduce pain perception and trigger positive feelings in the body. It's like getting a natural high minus the questionable life choices. Regular exercise can significantly decrease symptoms of depression and anxiety (Sharma et al., 2006).

But it's not just about endorphins. Exercise also

- reduces stress hormones like cortisol and adrenaline.
- improves sleep quality (and we know good sleep = better mood).
- boosts self-esteem and confidence.
- provides a healthy distraction from negative thoughts.
- increases social interaction if you exercise with others.

How Much Exercise Do You Need?

Now, before you start planning your Olympic training regimen, relax. You don't need to exercise for hours every day to reap the mental health benefits. The CDC recommends 150 minutes of moderate-intensity aerobic activity or 75 minutes of vigorous-intensity aerobic activity per week for adults (Centers for Disease Control and Prevention, 2023). But even small amounts of physical activity can make a difference.

Studies have found that people who exercised for 45 minutes three to five times a week had better mental health than those who didn't exercise (UCLA Health, 2018). But here's the cool part: More exercise wasn't necessarily better. People who exercised for more than 3 hours a day actually had worse mental health than those who didn't exercise at all. So, moderation is key!

Practical Tips for Getting Your Move On

1. Start small. A 10-minute walk is better than no walk at all. Remember, you're aiming for progress, not perfection.

2. Find an activity you enjoy. Dancing, swimming, hula hooping—if it gets you moving, it counts! Exercise doesn't have to feel like punishment.

3. Make it social. Join a sports team or work out with a friend. It's like multitasking for your mental health—you get the benefits of exercise and social connection.

4. Use the "just 5 minutes" rule. Tell yourself you'll exercise for just 5 minutes. Often, you'll end up doing more once you get started.

5. Incorporate movement into your daily routine. Take the stairs instead of the elevator, have walking meetings, or do some squats while you brush your teeth.

6. Try mindful exercise. Practices like yoga or tai chi combine physical activity with mindfulness, giving you a double dose of mental health benefits.

7. Get outside. Exercising in nature can provide additional mood-boosting benefits. It's like giving your brain a breath of fresh air—literally!

8. Celebrate your wins, no matter how small. Did a 5-minute yoga video? You're a fitness god/goddess! Acknowledging your efforts, no matter how small, can help build a positive association with exercise.

Remember, the best exercise is the one you'll actually do. So find what works for you and stick with it. Your mind (and body) will thank you!

Putting It All Together: Your Diet and Exercise Action Plan

Alright, now that we've stuffed your brain with all this knowledge about diet, exercise, and mental health, let's put it into action. Here's a simple 7-day plan to get you started:

- **Day 1:** Add one serving of fatty fish or nuts to your diet. Go for a 10-minute walk.

- **Day 2:** Swap one processed snack for a piece of fruit. Try a 5-minute yoga video.

- **Day 3:** Drink an extra glass of water. Do 10 jumping jacks every hour.

- **Day 4:** Add an extra serving of vegetables to your dinner. Dance to your favorite song.

- **Day 5:** Start your day with a protein-rich breakfast. Take a walk during your lunch break.

- **Day 6:** Try a new healthy recipe. Do some stretches while watching TV.

- **Day 7:** Have a mindful meal with no distractions. Try a new physical activity you've been curious about.

Please note: These are just suggestions. Feel free to adapt them to fit your life and preferences. The goal is to start making small, sustainable changes that can add up to big improvements in your mental health.

And hey, if you fall off the wagon (or the treadmill), don't beat yourself up. Every meal is a new opportunity to nourish your body, and every day is a new chance to move.

Optimizing Sleep to Calm an Overactive Negative Mind

Now, let's talk about the ultimate mood booster that I know a lot of us neglect: sleep. Yep, naps are actually good for your mental health. Who knew that being lazy could be so productive?

The Connection Between Sleep and Mental Health

Let's start with some cold, hard facts. A study by Walker (2009) found that sleep deprivation can seriously mess with our emotional processing. It's like trying to be positive while wearing cranky pants. Not a good look, folks.

Here's what happens when you don't get enough sleep (National Heart, Lung, and Blood Institute, 2022; Better Health Channel, n.d.):

- **Your amygdala goes into overdrive:** That's the part of your brain responsible for processing emotions. When you're sleep-deprived, it becomes more reactive to negative stimuli. It's like your brain is wearing nightmare-tinted glasses.

- **Your prefrontal cortex takes a nap:** This is the rational part of your brain that helps regulate those emotional responses. When you're tired, it's like your brain's responsible adult has left the building.

- **Your memory gets fuzzy:** Lack of sleep impairs your ability to remember positive emotional experiences. It's like your brain becomes a sieve, but it only catches the negative stuff.

- **Your decision-making skills go out the window:** Ever made a bad decision when you were tired? Blame it on your sleep-deprived brain. It's like trying to play chess while drunk—not a good idea.

Chronic lack of sleep isn't just making you grumpy in the short term. It's setting you up for some serious long-term mental health issues. Studies have shown that people with insomnia are at a higher risk of developing depression and anxiety disorders (Nutt et al., 2008).

Poor Sleep Intensifies Negative Thinking

Now, here's where things get really interesting (or frustrating, depending on how you look at it). Not only does lack of sleep lead to more negative thoughts, but negative thoughts can also lead to lack of sleep. It's the ultimate chicken-or-egg situation.

A study by Harvey (2002) found that people with insomnia tend to have more negative and intrusive thoughts when trying to fall asleep. We all know that feeling when our brain decides that bedtime is the perfect time to replay every embarrassing thing we've ever done or worry about that presentation next week.

This creates a vicious cycle:

1 You can't sleep because you're thinking negative thoughts.

2. You have more negative thoughts because you can't sleep.

3. Rinse and repeat.

It's like being on a really unpleasant merry-go-round that you can't get off. But don't worry, we're about to throw a wrench in those spinning gears!

Practical Strategies to Improve Sleep Quality

Here, we're going to turn your bedroom into a negativity-free zone. Here are some science-backed strategies to help you catch those much-needed Zs:

Cognitive Behavioral Therapy for Insomnia

This is the gold standard for treating insomnia without medication (Newsom & Dimitriu, 2024). Cognitive behavioral therapy for insomnia (CBT-I) involves:

- **Sleep restriction:** Limiting your time in bed to increase sleep efficiency.

- **Stimulus control:** Using your bed only for sleep and sex (sorry, no more Netflix in bed!).

- **Cognitive restructuring:** Challenging those pesky negative thoughts that keep you awake.

Mindfulness Meditation

Mindfulness can help calm that overactive mind of yours. Try this simple technique:

1. Focus on your breath.

2. When a thought pops up (and it will), acknowledge it without judgment.

3. Let the thought go and return your focus to your breath.

It's like giving your brain a mini-vacation from all that negative thinking.

Progressive Muscle Relaxation

This technique involves tensing and then relaxing each muscle group in your body. It's like giving yourself a full-body massage, minus the awkward small talk with a massage therapist.

The 4-7-8 Breathing Technique

Developed by Dr. Andrew Weil, this breathing exercise can help you fall asleep faster (WebMD Editorial Contributors, n.d.):

1. Exhale completely through your mouth.
2. Close your mouth and inhale quietly through your nose for 4 seconds.
3. Hold your breath for 7 seconds.
4. Exhale completely through your mouth for 8 seconds.
5. Repeat 3–4 times.

Case Study: Ishali's Sleep Transformation

Let's look at how these strategies worked for Ishali, a 35-year-old marketing executive who was caught in the negative thinking-poor sleep cycle.

Ishali's problem was that she would lie awake for hours, worrying about work and replaying conversations in her head. The next day, she would be exhausted and irritable, which only fueled more negative thoughts.

Her solution was to start CBT-I. She learned to challenge her negative thoughts and restrict her time in bed. She also incorporated a 10-minute mindfulness meditation into her bedtime routine.

After six weeks, Ishali fell asleep faster and stayed asleep longer. She reported feeling more positive and energetic during the day, and her colleagues noticed she was more upbeat at work.

Ishali's experience showed that better sleep really can lead to a more positive mindset!

Creating an Optimal Sleep Environment

So, how can you adjust your sleep environment and turn your bedroom into a negativity-free zone?

- **Keep it dark:** Your body produces melatonin (the sleep hormone) in darkness. Use blackout curtains or an eye mask to block out light. It's like creating a cave for your inner sleep bear.

- **Cool it down:** The ideal sleep temperature is around 65°F (18°C). If your room is too warm, your body can't cool down enough to induce sleep. It's like trying to sleep in a sauna—not fun.

- **Invest in comfort:** A comfortable mattress and pillows can make a world of difference. It's like the Goldilocks principle—not too hard, not too soft, but just right.

- **White noise is your friend:** If outside noises are keeping you up, try a white noise machine or app. It's like a sound blanket for your brain.

- **Make it a no-tech zone:** The blue light from screens can interfere with your melatonin production. Try to avoid screens for at least an hour before bed. It's like giving your brain a digital detox every night.

Lifestyle Changes for Better Sleep

Your daytime habits can have a big impact on your nighttime sleep. Here are some tips:

- **Stick to a sleep schedule:** Try to go to bed and wake up at the same time every day, even on weekends. Your body loves routine (Pacheco, 2023).

- **Create a bedtime ritual:** A relaxing routine can signal to your body that it's time to wind down. This could include reading, gentle stretching, or a warm bath (Pacheco, 2023).

- **Watch your caffeine intake:** Caffeine can stay in your system for up to eight hours. Try to cut it off by early afternoon.

- **Exercise regularly:** But not too close to bedtime. A good workout can help you sleep better, but not if it's right before bed.

- **Manage stress:** Try journaling before bed to get those worries out of your head and onto paper.

- **Avoid heavy meals late at night:** Your digestive system needs time to wind down, too.

Your Seven-Day Sleep Improvement Challenge

Are you ready to put all this into practice? Here's a seven-day plan to kickstart your journey to better sleep and more positive thinking:

- **Day 1:** Start a sleep diary. Record when you go to bed, when you wake up, and how you feel during the day.

- **Day 2:** Create a relaxing bedtime routine. Try reading or gentle stretching for 15 minutes before bed.

- **Day 3:** Make your bedroom a sleep sanctuary. Remove clutter, invest in comfortable bedding, and block out light and noise.

- **Day 4:** Cut off caffeine after 2 p.m. and avoid heavy meals within 3 hours of bedtime.

- **Day 5:** Try a 10-minute mindfulness meditation before bed.

- **Day 6:** Practice the 4-7-8 breathing technique when you get into bed.

- **Day 7:** Reflect on your sleep diary and note any improvements. Celebrate your progress!

Sweet dreams, and here's to waking up on the right side of the bed!

Creating a Positive Environment

If you're wondering what your messy coffee table has to do with your mental state, this section is for you. Here, we're going to learn how to create a space that makes your brain do a happy dance every time you walk through the door.

Importance of a Positive Environment

Studies have found that our physical surroundings can significantly impact our mental state (Meidenbauer, 2022). It's like your space is constantly whispering to your subconscious. Make sure it's saying nice things! Not only that, but our environment can influence our emotions.

It turns out that a positive environment can help reduce negative thoughts, stress, and anxiety.

So, what does this mean for you? Well, it's time to start thinking of your home as more than just a place to store your stuff and binge-watch Netflix.

Role of Physical Space

The layout and design of your space can have a big impact on your well-being. It's not just about making things look pretty (though that doesn't hurt); it's about creating a space that supports your mental health.

Here are some general principles to keep in mind:

- **Create zones:** Designate specific areas for work, relaxation, and sleep. This helps your brain switch gears more easily. It's like giving your mind a roadmap for the day.

- **Maximize natural light:** Sunlight is nature's mood booster. Try to arrange your space to get as much natural light as possible. If you're in a cave-like apartment, consider a light therapy lamp.

- **Declutter:** A cluttered space leads to a cluttered mind. We'll dive deeper into this later, but for now, remember: everything should have a home.

- **Bring nature indoors:** Plants aren't just pretty; they can actually improve air quality and boost mood. It's like having a little slice of forest bathing in your living room.

- **Create a cozy corner:** Designate a specific spot for relaxation. Whether it's a comfy chair for reading or a meditation cushion, having a go-to calm spot can work wonders.

Using Personal Belongings and Decorations

Surrounding ourselves with meaningful personal items can also significantly boost our life satisfaction. It's like each cherished object is a little happiness booster.

Here are some tips for infusing your space with personal joy:

- **Display happy memories:** Frame photos of good times or loved ones. It's like having a gallery of your greatest hits.

- **Showcase your passions:** Whether it's a bookshelf full of your favorite reads or a wall of your own artwork, surround yourself with things that represent what you love.

- **Incorporate sensory pleasures:** Think scented candles, soft throw blankets, or a speaker for your favorite tunes. Engage all your senses in creating a positive atmosphere.

- **Bring in nature:** We mentioned plants earlier, but this could also mean seashells from a favorite beach trip or a beautiful landscape painting.

- **Rotate your displays:** Keep things fresh by changing up your decor seasonally. It's like giving your space (and your mood) a regular refresh.

The goal is to create a space that makes you smile every time you look around. If an item doesn't bring you joy or serve a purpose, it might be time to thank it for its service and let it go.

Impact of Colors

I'm sure we've all struggled with choosing colors while redecorating. Colors can have a significant impact on our psychological function. Here's a quick rundown of how different colors might affect your mood:

- **Blue:** Calming and serene. Great for bedrooms or bathrooms.

- **Green:** Associated with nature and renewal. Perfect for a home office or living room.

- **Yellow:** Energizing and cheerful. Use it in small doses, like in a kitchen or entryway.

- **Red:** Stimulating and exciting. Best used as an accent color, not for an entire room (unless you want your space to feel like a bullfighting arena).

- **Purple:** Often associated with luxury and creativity. It could be great for a craft room or reading nook.

- **White:** Clean and fresh, but can feel cold in large doses. Balance it with warm accents.

- **Gray:** Neutral and sophisticated, but can be depressing if overused. Pair it with vibrant accents.

When choosing colors for your space, think about how you want to feel in each room. Want a calm bedroom? Go for cool, soothing tones. Need an energizing home office? Try warmer, more vibrant hues.

And remember, you don't have to paint entire rooms to get the benefits of color psychology. Throw pillows, artwork, or even a colorful rug can inject the right mood into your space.

Cleanliness and Organization

Last but definitely not least, let's talk about all the stuff crowding your room. Clutter can have a significant negative impact on our psychological home environment and subjective well-being. In other words, mess equals stress.

Here's why keeping your space clean and organized is crucial for a positive environment:

- **Reduces stress:** A tidy space means less visual distraction and stress.

- **Increases productivity:** When everything has a place, you spend less time searching and more time doing.

- **Improves sleep:** A clean, uncluttered bedroom can lead to better sleep quality.

- **Boosts mood:** The sense of accomplishment from a clean space can be a real mood lifter.

If you're currently thinking that cleaning is such a chore, take a look at the following practical tips to help make tidying less painful.

- **The two-minute rule:** If a task takes less than two minutes (like putting away dishes or hanging up a coat), do it immediately.

- **One in, one out:** For every new item you bring into your home, remove one.

- **Daily reset:** Spend 10 minutes each evening resetting your main living areas. It's like giving your space a mini-makeover every day.

- **Storage solutions:** Invest in good storage options. Baskets, drawer organizers, and under-bed storage can be game-changers.

- **Regular purges:** Schedule regular decluttering sessions. Be ruthless; if you haven't used it in a year, it might be time to let it go.

Your Seven-Day Challenge

Here's a plan to get you started:

- **Day 1:** Declutter one small area (like a drawer or shelf).
- **Day 2:** Add a plant or nature-inspired element to your main living area.
- **Day 3:** Create a cozy corner for relaxation.
- **Day 4:** Incorporate a new color into your space (even if it's just a throw pillow).
- **Day 5:** Display a few items that bring back happy memories.
- **Day 6:** Do a 20-minute clean sweep of your main living area.
- **Day 7:** Rearrange one room to maximize natural light and flow.

Creating a positive environment is an ongoing process. It's about continually curating a space that supports your mental health and well-being.

Key Takeaways and What's Next

This has been another really detailed and impactful chapter. We've talked about what you put in your mouth, how you move your body, catching those Zs, and how to spruce up your space. The main focus has been learning how your lifestyle can support positive thinking.

Start small, be consistent, and celebrate your progress along the way. Here's a quick action plan to get you started:

1. Add one mood-boosting food to your diet this week.

2. Try a new form of exercise, even if it's just a 10-minute dance party in your living room.

3. Set a consistent bedtime for the next week.

4. Declutter one small area of your home.

Now that we've set up your lifestyle for positivity success, it's time to learn from the pros. In our next chapter, we'll explore the habits of highly positive people. You're going to meet your inner optimist!

Chapter 15:

Adopting the Habits of Highly Positive People

It's time to learn about the habits of highly positive people. You can think of this chapter as a cheat sheet for happiness. We're going to uncover the secrets of those annoyingly cheerful people who seem to float through life on a cloud of rainbows and unicorns. Don't worry; this chapter won't make you annoying, just happier!

Understanding Positivity

Before we start imitating the happiness gurus, let's talk about what positivity really means. It's not about walking around with a permanent grin plastered on your face or pretending everything's peachy keen when it's clearly not. Nope, true positivity is about maintaining a realistic yet optimistic outlook on life, even when things get tough.

Positivity isn't just a feel-good buzzword; it's a powerful force that can significantly impact your mental and physical health. Don't believe me? Let's look at some cold, hard science.

A study by Cohen et al. (2003) found that people with a more positive emotional style had lower levels of cortisol (the stress hormone) and were less likely to catch a cold. Yep, positivity might actually boost your immune system. It's a superhero for your health.

Positivity has also been linked to (Kubzansky et al., 2001; Musich et al., 2022):

- better cardiovascular health

- improved mental health

- higher resilience to stress
- stronger relationships
- increased longevity

Characteristics and Habits of Highly Positive People

Now that we know why positivity is so important, let's look at the traits that make up these walking rays of sunshine. What sets them apart from the Debbie Downers and Negative Nancys of the world?

- **Optimism:** This is the heavy hitter of positivity. Optimists expect good things to happen and interpret events in a positive light. It's like they're wearing rose-colored glasses, but ones that actually improve their vision.

- **Resilience:** Positive people bounce back from setbacks faster than a rubber ball on steroids. They see challenges as opportunities for growth rather than insurmountable obstacles.

- **Gratitude:** These folks could find something to be thankful for in a hurricane. They appreciate the good in their lives, big and small.

- **Mindfulness:** Positive people tend to be present in the moment rather than dwelling on the past or worrying about the future. It's like they're time travelers, but they choose to stay in the now.

- **Solution-focused:** Instead of complaining about problems, they look for ways to solve them.

- **Empathy:** Positive people tend to be more in tune with others' emotions and more willing to lend a helping hand. They're like emotional sponges, but in a good way.

- **Self-compassion:** They treat themselves with the same kindness they'd show a good friend.

If you weren't born with those traits... me too! Most people aren't. These are characteristics that can be developed and strengthened over time. And the benefits are more than just feeling good. A study by Boehm et al. (2011) found that positive psychological well-being actually reduces the risk of heart disease.

Practical Steps to Adopt These Habits

Now, let's roll up our sleeves and get to work on building these positive habits. Again, this is not an overnight transformation. You can think of this more like a gradual makeover for your mind.

Cultivating Optimism

- **Reframe negative thoughts:** When you catch yourself thinking negatively, challenge that thought. Is it really true? Is there another way to look at the situation?

- **Practice gratitude:** Start or end each day by noting three things you're grateful for. They can be big (got a promotion!) or small (found a parking spot right away).

- **Focus on solutions:** When faced with a problem, ask yourself, "What can I do about this?" instead of "Why does this always happen to me?"

- **Limit negative media exposure:** While it's important to stay informed, constant exposure to negative news can be a real downer. Try setting boundaries on your news consumption.

- **Help others:** Doing good for others can help you feel more positive about the world and your place in it. It's like karma but with a faster turnaround time.

Building Resilience

- **Maintain good relationships:** Strong social connections provide support during tough times. It's like having a personal cheerleading squad.

- **Accept change:** Remember, change is the only constant in life. Embracing it rather than resisting it can reduce stress.

- **Learn from past experiences:** Instead of dwelling on past mistakes, think about what they taught you. Turn your life into a series of teachable moments.

- **Develop problem-solving skills:** Break big problems into smaller, manageable steps. It's like eating an elephant—one bite at a time (not that we recommend eating elephants, mind you).

- **Take care of yourself:** Regular exercise, healthy eating, and adequate sleep can boost your resilience.

Practicing Gratitude

- **Keep a gratitude journal:** Write down three things you're grateful for each day. Don't worry if they seem small—even "had a great cup of coffee" counts!

- **Express thankfulness regularly:** Tell people in your life why you appreciate them. Sprinkle a little bit of happiness confetti everywhere you go.

- **Celebrate small wins:** Accomplished a task on your to-do list? Give yourself a mental high five!

- **Use visual reminders:** Put up sticky notes with things you're grateful for, or set reminders on your phone. It's like leaving little gifts for your future self to find.

- **Practice mindful gratitude:** Really savor positive experiences when they happen. It's like hitting the "save" button on happy moments in your mental computer.

Your Seven-Day Challenge

If you're ready to start putting all these things into action, you can get started with this seven-day challenge:

- **Day 1:** Write down three things you're grateful for.

- **Day 2:** Reframe one negative thought into a more positive or balanced perspective.

- **Day 3:** Do one small act of kindness for someone else.

- **Day 4:** Spend 10 minutes problem-solving a current challenge in your life.

- **Day 5:** Reach out to a friend or family member you appreciate and tell them why.

- **Day 6:** Try a new stress-reduction technique (like deep breathing or progressive muscle relaxation).

- **Day 7:** Celebrate three small wins from your week.

Key Takeaways and What's Next

Here's a quick recap of what we've covered in this chapter:

- Positivity isn't just about feeling good; it has real, measurable impacts on your mental and physical health.

- Highly positive people share common traits like optimism, resilience, and gratitude.

- These traits aren't just for the chosen few; they can be developed and strengthened over time.

- Practical steps like reframing negative thoughts, building strong relationships, and practicing gratitude can help you adopt these positive habits.

Becoming more positive isn't about ignoring the negative aspects of life or pretending everything is perfect. It's about developing a more balanced, optimistic outlook that helps you navigate life's ups and downs with greater ease and resilience.

Now that we've learned how to adopt the habits of highly positive people, it's time to talk about how to maintain this positivity long-term. In our next (and final) chapter together, we'll explore strategies for dealing with negative thought relapses and the importance of building a strong support system. Even the sunniest of dispositions can have a few clouds roll in now and then!

Chapter 16:

Negative Thought Relapses and Building a Support System

Throughout the book so far, you've learned many tools, skills, and techniques to help you combat negative thinking. However, sometimes those pesky negative thoughts stage a comeback tour in your mind. These are tough relapses. It's like whack-a-mole but with thoughts.

I won't leave you hanging, though. We're also going to talk about your secret weapon in this ongoing battle: your support system. This is like assembling your very own superhero team who can help you battle negative thoughts.

Understanding Negative Thought Relapses

So, what do we mean by a negative thought relapse? It's when those old patterns of negativity (that you've been working so hard to change) decide to make an unwelcome reappearance. It's when you feel like you've taken two steps forward and one step back: You've been doing great, thinking positively, and seeing the glass half full... and then bam! Suddenly, you're back to your old negative thought patterns.

Why do these pesky relapses happen? Well, there are a few reasons:

- **Stress:** When we're under pressure, our brains often default to old, familiar patterns—like comfort food, but for your mind. Studies have found that stress can reactivate negative cognitive schemas (Krkovic et al., 2018). Stress can be the key that unlocks the door to your negative thought vault.

- **Lack of sleep:** Remember how we talked about the importance of sleep? When we're tired, our mental defenses are down, making it easier for negative thoughts to sneak in. Studies have found that poor sleep quality is associated with increased negative thinking (Scott et al., 2021).

- **Not maintaining positive habits:** Sometimes, we get complacent and stop practicing the techniques we've learned. It's like expecting to stay fit after stopping your gym routine. A study by Hoorelbeke and Koster (2017) found that stopping cognitive control training led to increased negative thinking in people who had recovered from depression.

- **Major life changes:** Big transitions can throw us off balance and trigger old thought patterns. Major life events can trigger depressive episodes, even in people who have been well for a while.

- **Biological factors:** Sometimes, it's not just about what's happening in your life, but what's happening in your body. Hormonal changes, for example, can influence mood and thought patterns.

Identifying Signs of Negative Thought Relapses

How do you know if you're experiencing a relapse? Here are some signs to watch out for:

- increased feelings of anxiety or depression
- returning to old coping mechanisms (like overeating or excessive drinking)
- difficulty sleeping or changes in sleep patterns
- increased irritability or mood swings
- negative self-talk that becomes more frequent

- avoiding social situations or withdrawing from friends and family

- decreased motivation or loss of interest in activities you usually enjoy

- physical symptoms like headaches or stomach aches with no clear medical cause

- difficulty concentrating or making decisions

- feeling overwhelmed by tasks that you previously managed well

Strategies for Managing Negative Thought Relapses

So you've spotted the signs of a relapse. Now what? Here are some evidence-based strategies to help you manage:

- **Mindfulness:** Take a few minutes each day to practice mindfulness. It's like hitting the pause button on your negative thought spiral. Khoury et al. (2015) found that mindfulness-based interventions were effective in reducing symptoms of anxiety and depression.

- **Journaling:** Write down your thoughts and feelings. It's like being your own therapist but with worse handwriting. Krpan et al. (2013) found that expressive writing can help reduce depressive symptoms.

- **Reach out:** This is where your support system comes in. Don't try to weather the storm alone. Social support has been found to be associated with better mental health outcomes (Gariépy et al., 2016).

- **Review your toolbox:** Go back to the strategies we've discussed in earlier chapters. It's like reviewing your notes before an exam, but the exam is life.

- **Self-compassion:** Remember, relapses are normal. Don't beat yourself up over it. Treat yourself with the same kindness you'd show a friend.

- **Physical exercise:** Get moving! Research has found that exercise can help prevent depression (Schuch et al., 2019).

Maintaining Positivity During a Relapse

Even during a relapse, there are ways to maintain a sense of positivity:

- **Practice gratitude:** Every day, try to identify three things you're grateful for, no matter how small.

- **Focus on small wins:** Celebrate your small achievements. Finished a task at work? That's a win! Got out of bed on a tough day? Also, a win!

- **Engage in pleasant activities:** Do things you enjoy, even if you don't feel like it at first.

- **Practice positive self-talk:** Challenge your negative thoughts with positive affirmations.

- **Visualize success:** Imagine yourself overcoming this relapse.

Real-Life Relapse Warriors

Let's hear from a couple of people who've successfully navigated their own negative thought relapses:

Sarah's story: Sarah, a 34-year-old teacher, experienced a relapse after a stressful period at work. "I found myself falling back into old patterns of self-doubt and anxiety," she says. "But I remembered the techniques I'd learned. I started journaling every night and practiced mindfulness during my lunch breaks. It wasn't easy, but after a few weeks, I started feeling more like myself again. The key was not giving up, even on the tough days."

Michael's journey: Michael, a 45-year-old accountant, faced a relapse after a major life change. "When I got divorced, all my old negative thoughts came flooding back," he shares. "But I reached out to my support system and started seeing a therapist again. I also made sure to exercise every day, even if it was just a short walk. Slowly but surely, I started to see the light at the end of the tunnel. Now, I know that even if I have a relapse, I have the tools to get through it."

It's important to remind yourself that relapse doesn't erase all the progress you've made. It's just a detour on your journey to more positive thinking. With the right strategies and support, you can navigate these challenging periods and come out stronger on the other side.

What Is a Support System?

Now, let's discuss your secret weapon in the fight against negative thinking: your support system. Let's dive into what exactly we mean by a "support system" and why it's crucial for your mental health journey.

Understanding the Concept of a Support System

A support system is essentially your personal network of people who provide emotional and practical support. It's like having a team of emotional bodyguards ready to back you up when negativity tries to crash your mental party. This network can include:

- **Family:** The people who've known you since you were in diapers (and love you anyway).

- **Friends:** Your chosen family, the ones who stick with you through thick and thin.

- **Romantic partners:** Your significant other, who's signed up for front-row seats to your life's roller coaster.

- **Mentors:** The wise sages who guide you through life's trickier moments.

- **Coworkers:** The allies who help you navigate the 9-to-5 jungle.

- **Mental health professionals:** Therapists, counselors, and other professionals who provide expert support.

- **Support groups:** Fellow travelers on similar journeys, offering understanding and camaraderie.

- **Online communities:** Digital tribes that provide support across distances.

- **Pets:** Yes, really! Your furry (or scaly or feathery) friends can be a crucial part of your support system.

Having a support system really makes a difference. Umberson and Karas Montez (2010) found that social relationships have a significant impact on mental and physical health. It's like your relationships are a health tonic but way more fun.

Role of a Support System in Overcoming Negative Thinking

So, how exactly does a support system help you in your battle against negative thinking? Let me count the ways:

- **Perspective shifting:** When you're stuck in a negative thought spiral, your support system can offer fresh perspectives. It's like they're handing you a different pair of glasses to view your situation through.

- **Emotional validation:** Sometimes, you just need someone to acknowledge that what you're feeling is real and valid. Your support system can provide that validation, which can be incredibly reassuring during times of stress or anxiety.

- **Problem-solving support:** Two (or more) heads are often better than one when it comes to tackling life's challenges. Your support system can offer ideas and solutions you might not have thought of on your own.

- **Distraction and fun:** Sometimes, the best way to combat negative thoughts is to take a break from them altogether. Your support system can provide much-needed distraction and inject some fun into your life.

- **Accountability:** When you're trying to change thought patterns, it can be helpful to have someone to check in with. Your support system can help keep you accountable for your mental health goals.

Perceived social support has been found to be linked to lower rates of depression and anxiety. It's like your support system is a shield, deflecting those pesky negative thoughts.

Identifying and Building Your Own Support System

Now that you know why a support system is crucial, let's talk about how to build and strengthen yours:

- **Identify your current supporters:** Who do you turn to when things get tough? These are your MVP supporters. Make a list—you might be surprised at how many people are already in your corner.

- **Diversify your network:** Don't rely on just one or two people. It's like having a diversified investment portfolio but for emotional support. Aim to have supporters from different areas of your life.

- **Be proactive:** Don't wait for a crisis to reach out. Regular check-ins with your support network can strengthen these relationships over time.

- **Be a good supporter:** Remember, support is a two-way street. Be there for others, and they're more likely to be there for you. It's like emotional karma.

- **Set boundaries:** Healthy relationships have boundaries. It's okay to let your supporters know what kind of help you need (and don't need).

- **Consider professional help:** Sometimes, you need a pro. There's no shame in seeking help from a therapist or counselor. It's like hiring a personal trainer for your mind.

- **Join support groups:** Whether online or in-person, support groups can provide understanding and camaraderie. Find your emotional tribe.

- **Nurture new connections:** Be open to new friendships and relationships. You never know who might become a valuable part of your support system.

- **Utilize technology:** In our digital age, support can come through a screen. Use social media, video calls, and messaging apps to stay connected with your support network.

Benefits of Having a Strong Support System

Having a strong support system isn't just nice to have; it's crucial for your mental health. Here's why:

- **Stress reduction:** A study by Southwick et al. (2014) found that social support significantly contributes to resilience against psychological stress. It's like having an emotional shock absorber.

- **Improved mood:** As mentioned earlier, research has shown that perceived social support is associated with lower levels of depression and anxiety (Grey et al., 2020).

- **Better coping skills:** Individuals with strong social support tend to use more effective coping strategies during stressful times.

- **Increased self-esteem:** Supportive relationships can boost self-esteem and self-worth.

- **Longer life:** Believe it or not, strong social connections are associated with longevity. Studies have found that people with stronger social relationships had a 50% increased likelihood of survival compared to those with weaker social relationships (Holt-Lunstad et al., 2010).

- **Faster recovery:** When you do experience setbacks or health issues, a strong support system can help you recover faster. A study found that cardiac patients with higher perceived social support had better recovery outcomes (Wenn et al., 2022).

- **Increased sense of belonging:** Feeling connected to others fulfills a basic human need. Research found that a sense of belonging is crucial for mental health and well-being (Haim-Litevsky et al., 2023).

Now that you know why a support network is so important for you in battling your negative thinking, go forth and work on your support network! It's a bit like tending a garden—it needs regular care and attention to flourish.

Your Seven-Day Support System Challenge

Ready to strengthen your support network? Here's a 7-day challenge:

- **Day 1:** Identify three people in your current support system.
- **Day 2:** Reach out to someone you haven't talked to in a while.
- **Day 3:** Practice active listening with a friend or family member.
- **Day 4:** Research local support groups or online communities related to your interests or challenges.
- **Day 5:** Do something kind for someone in your support network.
- **Day 6:** Share a struggle you're facing with someone you trust.
- **Day 7:** Reflect on how your support system has helped you this week.

Key Takeaways

Let's recap what we've learned in this chapter:

- Negative thought relapses are normal and don't mean you've failed.
- Recognize the signs early and use your tools to manage relapses.

- Build and maintain a diverse support system.

- Don't hesitate to seek professional help when needed.

- Remember, having support isn't a sign of weakness; it's a sign of wisdom.

This journey isn't just about overcoming negative thinking; it's about creating a lifelong practice of positivity and resilience.

So, keep your support team close and your positivity tools closer, and remember: You've got this! And even when you don't feel like you've got this, you've got people who've got your back. Now that's something to feel positive about!

Conclusion

Well, well, well. Look at you! You made it to the end of this book, armed with a toolkit full of strategies to combat negative thinking. Give yourself a pat on the back, a high five, or maybe even treat yourself to that fancy coffee you've been eyeing. You deserve it!

But before you rush off to spread your newfound positivity to the world (and possibly blind unsuspecting bystanders with your radiant optimism), let's take a moment to reflect on the journey we've been on together.

Do you remember when we started? Your mind was probably a bit like a snow globe of negative thoughts—shake it up, and suddenly, you're in a blizzard of "I can't" and "What if." But now? Now, you're the master of your mental weather. You can't control every thought that drifts through your mind, but you've got the tools to decide which ones get to stay and set up camp. You should be pretty darn proud of yourself!

The Journey So Far: From Negativity Ninja to Positivity Pro

We dove deep into the murky waters of negative thinking, learning to spot those sneaky thought patterns that love to rain on our mental parade.

- We became thought detectives, identifying our own unique "negativity fingerprint" (turns out, it's not as cool as having a superpower, but identifying it is the first step to changing it!).
- We learned a whole arsenal of strategies to break free from negativity's grip—from cognitive behavioral techniques (fancy

words for "teaching your brain new tricks") to mindfulness practices (aka "being present without judgment, even when your mind is throwing a tantrum").

- We explored how to maintain this positive mindset for the long haul because, let's face it, becoming a positivity pro isn't a "one and done" deal. It's more like brushing your teeth—you gotta do it regularly, or things start to get a bit stinky.

- And finally, we learned about the power of a support system because even superheroes need sidekicks sometimes.

Key Points to Remember

Now let's take a look at the highlights of our positivity journey:

Understanding Negative Thinking: The Villain of Our Story

Remember, negative thoughts are like that one relative who always has something critical to say at family gatherings. They're going to show up, but you don't have to let them dominate the conversation. Negative thinking can amp up your stress and anxiety levels faster than a caffeinated squirrel, but now you know how to spot it and stop it.

Identifying Your Negative Thought Patterns: Know Thy Enemy

We've all got our favorite flavors of negative thinking. Maybe you're a catastrophizer, always imagining the worst-case scenario ("I'm going to be late to work, get fired, become homeless, and end up living in a cardboard box!"). Or perhaps you're an overgeneralizer, turning one setback into a life sentence ("I burnt the toast. I'm a terrible cook and a failure at life."). Recognizing these patterns is like catching your brain in the act of throwing a pessimism party.

Proven Strategies to Break Free of Negativity: Your Positivity Toolbox

We've stuffed your mental toolkit with all sorts of goodies:

- cognitive behavioral therapy techniques (teaching your brain to fact-check its own dramatic tendencies)

- mindfulness practices (being present in the moment, even when the moment kind of sucks)

- positive affirmations (personal pep talks that actually work)

- gratitude practices (appreciating the good stuff, even when life is serving you a sandwich of disappointment)

Maintaining a Positive Mindset Long-Term: The Marathon, Not the Sprint

Remember, becoming a positivity pro is not about never having a negative thought again (sorry, but unless you're a golden retriever, that's probably not going to happen). It's about building the mental muscles to handle those thoughts when they do pop up. Consistency is key; it's like going to the gym for your mind. You wouldn't expect to get buff after one workout, right? The same goes for your mental fitness.

Key Takeaways: All You Can Eat Wisdom

Here's a smorgasbord of takeaways from our journey together:

- Your thoughts are not facts. Just because you think it doesn't make it true (Chapter 1).

- You have the power to change your thought patterns. Your brain is like Play-Doh: endlessly moldable (Chapter 2).

- Mindfulness isn't just for Zen masters. It's for anyone who wants to be more aware of their thoughts and less controlled by them (Chapter 3).

- Gratitude is like a superhero cape for your mood. Wear it often (Chapter 4).

- Your environment affects your mindset. Surround yourself with positivity, both in your physical space and your relationships (Chapter 5).

- Self-compassion isn't selfish; it's necessary. Treat yourself like you would a good friend (Chapter 6).

- Resilience is a skill you can build, like a mental muscle. The more you practice, the stronger you get (Chapter 7).

- A support system isn't a luxury; it's a necessity. Don't go through life's challenges alone (Chapter 8).

- Relapses happen. It's not about never falling down; it's about how quickly you get back up (Chapter 9).

- Positivity is a practice, not a destination. Keep at it, and watch how it transforms your life (Chapter 10).

- Challenging negative thoughts with evidence is like being a detective in your own mind. Seek the facts, not just the feelings (Chapter 11).

- Reframing, visualization, and the "Yes, But" technique are powerful tools to flip the script on negative thinking. Use them liberally (Chapter 12).

- Your work life, relationships, body image, and finances all benefit from positive thinking. Apply these techniques in all areas of your life (Chapter 13).

- Your lifestyle choices, including diet, exercise, and sleep, play a crucial role in maintaining a positive mindset. Treat your body well to treat your mind well. (Chapter 14).

- Highly positive people aren't born; they're made. Adopt their habits, and you're on your way to joining their ranks (Chapter 15).

- Building a strong support system and knowing how to handle relapses are key to maintaining long-term positivity. You don't have to go it alone (Chapter 16).

Your Mission

All this knowledge is great and all, but it's about as useless as a chocolate teapot if you don't put it into practice, so here's your mission:

1. **Choose one strategy from this book to implement today.** Just one. Maybe it's a mindfulness practice, starting a gratitude journal, or giving yourself a daily pep talk in the mirror (yes, it feels silly at first, but so do most worthwhile things).

2. **Commit to practicing this strategy every day for a week.** Put a reminder in your phone, stick a note on your fridge, or tattoo it on your forehead (okay, maybe not that last one).

3. **At the end of the week, reflect on how it's affected your mood and thought patterns.** Give yourself a gold star for effort, regardless of the results.

4. **Rinse and repeat with other strategies from the book.** Before you know it, you'll be a walking, talking, positivity factory!

5. **When you hit a rough patch (and you will, because you're human and life likes to keep us on our toes), come back to this book.** Reread the chapters that resonate with you. Treat it like a pep talk from a friend who really wants you to succeed (because that's exactly what it is!).

A Small Favor (No Pressure, but Also Yes, Pressure)

If you found this book helpful—if it made you laugh, think, or see your thoughts in a new light—I'd be eternally grateful if you could leave a review. It helps other readers discover the book and spread more positivity in the world. And let's face it, the world could always use more positivity, right?

Plus, every time someone leaves a review, a unicorn gets its wings. (Okay, that's not true, but wouldn't it be cool if it was?).

Last Words

You have the power to shape your thoughts, and your thoughts have the power to shape your life. It won't always be easy, and there will be days when positivity feels as elusive as a cat when it's time to go to the vet. But keep at it. You're stronger than you think, more resilient than you know, and absolutely capable of creating a life filled with more positivity and less stress.

So go forth, spread those good vibes, and remember: Every time you choose a positive thought, you're making the world a little bit brighter. And if you find yourself with an overabundance of positivity? Well, feel free to send some my way. I accept payment in smiles, high-fives, and terrible puns.

Now get out there and show negativity who's boss. You've got this!

References

Ackerman, C. E. (2017, April 12). *Benefits of gratitude: 28+ surprising research findings*. PositivePsychology.com. https://positivepsychology.com/benefits-gratitude-research-questions/

Acoba, E. F. (2024). Social support and mental health: The mediating role of perceived stress. *Frontiers in Psychology, 15*. https://doi.org/10.3389/fpsyg.2024.1330720

APA. (2017). *What is cognitive behavioral therapy?* https://www.apa.org/ptsd-guideline/patients-and-families/cognitive-behavioral#:~:text=In%20many%20studies%2C%20CBT%20has

Arden, J., B. (2010). *Rewire your brain: Think your way to a better life*. Jossey Bass

Beau, A. (2021, May 26). *How to spot and swap the 4 types of negative self-talk*. Shine. https://advice.theshineapp.com/articles/how-to-spot-and-swap-the-4-types-of-negative-self-talk/

Beck, A. T., Rush, A. J., Shaw, B. F., & Emery, G. (1987). *Cognitive therapy of depression*. New York: Guilford Press.

Better Health Channel. (n.d.). *Sleep deprivation*. https://www.betterhealth.vic.gov.au/health/conditionsandtreatments/sleep-deprivation

Bevilacqua, L., & Goldman, D. (2011). Genetics of emotion. *Trends in Cognitive Sciences, 15*(9), 401–408. https://doi.org/10.1016/j.tics.2011.07.009

Boehm, J. K., Peterson, C., Kivimaki, M., & Kubzansky, L. (2011). A prospective study of positive psychological well-being and coronary heart disease. *Health Psychology, 30*(3), 259–267. https://doi.org/10.1037/a0023124

Burns, D., D. (1999). *Feeling good: The new mood therapy*. Avon Books.

Butler, A. C., Chapman, J. E., Forman, E. M., & Beck, A. T. (2006). The empirical status of cognitive-behavioral therapy: a review of meta-analyses. *Clinical Psychology Review, 26*(1), 17–31. https://doi.org/10.1016/j.cpr.2005.07.003

Carrière, K., Khoury, B., Günak, M. M., & Knäuper, B. (2018). Mindfulness-based interventions for weight loss: A systematic review and meta-analysis. *Obesity Reviews, 19*(2), 164–177. https://doi.org/10.1111/obr.12623

Casad, B. J., & Luebering, J. E. (2024, July 30). Confirmation bias. In *Encyclopedia Britannica.* https://www.britannica.com/science/confirmation-bias

Cascio, C. N., O'Donnell, M. B., Tinney, F. J., Lieberman, M. D., Taylor, S. E., Strecher, V. J., & Falk, E. B. (2016). Self-affirmation activates brain systems associated with self-related processing and reward and is reinforced by future orientation. *Social Cognitive and Affective Neuroscience, 11*(4), 621–629. https://doi.org/10.1093/scan/nsv136

Celestine, N. (2020, August 15). *What is mindful breathing? Exercises, scripts, and videos.* PositivePsychology.com. https://positivepsychology.com/mindful-breathing/

Centers for Disease Control and Prevention. (2023, December 6). *What counts as physical activity for adults.* https://www.cdc.gov/physical-activity-basics/adding-adults/what-counts.html#:~:text=Each%20week%2C%20adults%20should%20aim

Cherry, K. (2024, May 7). How cognitive biases influence the way you think and act. Verywell Mind. https://www.verywellmind.com/what-is-a-cognitive-bias-2794963

Cohen, S., Doyle, W. J., Turner, R. B., Alper, C. M., & Skoner, D. P. (2003). Emotional style and susceptibility to the common cold. *Psychosomatic Medicine, 65*(4), 652–657. https://doi.org/10.1097/01.psy.0000077508.57784.da

Cohen, S., Janicki-Deverts, D., Doyle, W. J., Miller, G. E., Frank, E., Rabin, B. S., & Turner, R. B. (2012). Chronic stress, glucocorticoid receptor resistance, inflammation, and disease risk. *Proceedings of the National Academy of Sciences, 109*(16), 5995–5999. https://doi.org/10.1073/pnas.1118355109

Cuncic, A. (2020, June 29). *How to stop negative thoughts.* Verywell Mind. https://www.verywellmind.com/how-to-change-negative-thinking-3024843

Davidson, R. J., & McEwen, B. S. (2012). Social influences on neuroplasticity: Stress and interventions to promote well-being. *Nature Neuroscience, 15,* 689–695. https://doi.org/10.1038/nn.3093

Dean, J. (2024, February 20). *For couples, negative speaks louder than positive.* Phys.org. https://phys.org/news/2024-02-couples-negative-louder-positive.html#:~:text=New%20Cornell%20psychology%20research%20finds

Eagleson, C., Hayes, S., Mathews, A., Perman, G., & Hirsch, C. R. (2016). The power of positive thinking: Pathological worry is reduced by thought replacement in Generalized Anxiety Disorder. *Behaviour Research and Therapy, 78,* 13–18. https://doi.org/10.1016/j.brat.2015.12.017

Emmons, R. A., & McCullough, M. E. (2003). Counting blessings versus burdens: An experimental investigation of gratitude and subjective well-being in daily life. *Journal of Personality & Social Psychology, 84*(2), 377–389. https://doi.org/10.1037//0022-3514.84.2.377

Epstein, N., & Baucom, D. H. (2002). *Enhanced cognitive-behavioral therapy for couples: A contextual approach.* American Psychological Association.

Everaert, J., Podina, I. R., & Koster, E. H. W. (2017). A comprehensive meta-analysis of interpretation biases in depression. *Clinical Psychology Review, 58,* 33–48. https://doi.org/10.1016/j.cpr.2017.09.005

Feeney, B. C., & Collins, N. L. (2015). A new look at social support: A theoretical perspective on thriving through relationships. *Personality* and *Social Psychology Review, 19*(2), 113–147. https://doi.org/10.1177/1088868314544222

Ferrara, E., & Yang, Z. (2015). Measuring emotional contagion in social media. *PLOS ONE, 10*(11), e0142390. https://doi.org/10.1371/journal.pone.0142390

Frank, C., Land, W. M., Popp, C., & Schack, T. (2014). Mental representation and mental practice: Experimental investigation on the functional links between motor memory and motor imagery. *PLoS ONE, 9*(4), e95175. https://doi.org/10.1371/journal.pone.0095175

Fredrickson, B. L., Cohn, M. A., Coffey, K. A., Pek, J., & Finkel, S. M. (2008). Open hearts build lives: Positive emotions, induced through loving-kindness meditation, build consequential personal resources. *Journal of Personality and Social Psychology, 95*(5), 1045–1062. https://doi.org/10.1037/a0013262

Frewen, P. A., Dozois, D. J. A., Neufeld, R. W. J., & Lanius, R. A. (2008). Meta-analysis of alexithymia in posttraumatic stress disorder. *Journal of Traumatic Stress, 21*(2), 243–246. https://doi.org/10.1002/jts.20320

Fritscher, L. (2023, October 31). *How to use thought stopping techniques to control unwanted thoughts*. Verywell Mind. https://www.verywellmind.com/stop-technique-2671653#:~:text=Thought%20stopping%20is%20a%20strategy

Gariépy, G., Honkaniemi, H., & Quesnel-Vallée, A. (2016). Social support and protection from depression: Systematic review of current findings in Western countries. *British Journal of Psychiatry, 209*(4), 284–293. https://doi.org/10.1192/bjp.bp.115.169094

Gibbon, P. (2020). *Martin Seligman and the rise of positive psychology*. National Endowment for the Humanities (NEH). https://www.neh.gov/article/martin-seligman-and-rise-positive-psychology

Goldberg, S. B., Tucker, R. P., Greene, P. A., Davidson, R. J., Wampold, B. E., Kearney, D. J., & Simpson, T. L. (2018). Mindfulness-based interventions for psychiatric disorders: A systematic review and meta-

analysis. *Clinical Psychology Review, 59,* 52–60.
https://doi.org/10.1016/j.cpr.2017.10.011

Grey, I., Arora, T., Thomas, J., Saneh, A., Tohme, P., & Abi-Habib, R. (2020). The role of perceived social support on depression and sleep during the COVID-19 pandemic. *Psychiatry Research, 293,* 113452. https://doi.org/10.1016/j.psychres.2020.113452

Haim-Litevsky, D., Komemi, R., & Lipskaya-Velikovsky, L. (2023). Sense of belonging, meaningful daily life participation, and well-being: Integrated investigation. *International Journal of Environmental Research and Public Health, 20*(5), 4121.
https://doi.org/10.3390/ijerph20054121

Hankin, B. L., Abramson, L. Y., Miller, N., & Haeffel, G. J. (2004). Cognitive vulnerability-stress theories of depression: Examining affective specificity in the prediction of depression versus anxiety in three prospective studies. *Cognitive Therapy and Research, 28,* 309–345. https://doi.org/10.1023/b:cotr.0000031805.60529.0d

Hanson, R. (2013). *Hardwiring happiness: The new brain science of contentment, calm, and confidence.* Harmony.

Harvard University. (n.d.). *Identifying negative automatic thought patterns.* https://sdlab.fas.harvard.edu/cognitive-reappraisal/identifying-negative-automatic-thought-patterns

Harvey, A. G. (2002). A cognitive model of insomnia. *Behaviour Research and Therapy, 40*(8), 869–893. https://doi.org/10.1016/s0005-7967(01)00061-4

Hoffman, S. G., & Smits, J. A. J. (2008). Cognitive-behavioral therapy for adult anxiety disorders: A meta-analysis of randomized placebo-controlled trials. *The Journal of Clinical Psychiatry.* https://doi.org/10.4088/jcp.v69n0415

Hofmann, S. G., Asnaani, A., Vonk, I. J. J., Sawyer, A. T., & Fang, A. (2012). The efficacy of cognitive behavioral therapy: A review of meta-analyses. *Cognitive Therapy and Research, 36,* 427–440. https://doi.org/10.1007/s10608-012-9476-1

Holt-Lunstad, J., Smith, T. B., & Layton, J. B. (2010). Social relationships and mortality risk: A meta-analytic review. *PLoS Medicine, 7*(7), e1000316. https://journals.plos.org/plosmedicine/article?id=10.1371/journal.pmed.1000316

Hölzel, B. K., Carmody, J., Vangel, M., Congleton, C., Yerramsetti, S. M., Gard, T., & Lazar, S. W. (2011). Mindfulness practice leads to increases in regional brain gray matter density. *Psychiatry Research: Neuroimaging, 191*(1), 36–43. https://doi.org/10.1016/j.pscychresns.2010.08.006

Hoorelbeke, K., & Koster, E. H. W. (2017). Internet-delivered cognitive control training as a preventive intervention for remitted depressed patients: Evidence from a double-blind randomized controlled trial study. *Journal of Consulting and Clinical Psychology, 85*(2), 135–146. https://doi.org/10.1037/ccp0000128

How to use CBT thought records to change the way you feel. (n.d.). Psychology Tools. https://www.psychologytools.com/self-help/thought-records/

Kamel, G. (2023, December 12). *How the debt snowball method works.* Ramsey Solutions. https://www.ramseysolutions.com/debt/how-the-debt-snowball-method-works?srsltid=AfmBOoox7vuVs5DOcrbREDMq9rEoHJJpdSPBAffr0QsnNKCruxkLFZG1

Khoury, B., Sharma, M., Rush, S. E., & Fournier, C. (2015). Mindfulness-based stress reduction for healthy individuals: A meta-analysis. *Journal of Psychosomatic Research, 78*(6), 519–528. https://doi.org/10.1016/j.jpsychores.2015.03.009

Komase, Y., Watanabe, K., Hori, D., Nozawa, K., Hidaka, Y., Iida, M., Imamura, K., & Kawakami, N. (2021). Effects of gratitude intervention on mental health and well-being among workers: A systematic review. *Journal of Occupational Health, 63*(1), e12290. https://doi.org/10.1002/1348-9585.12290

Krantz, S., & Hammen, C. L. (1979). Assessment of cognitive bias in depression. *Journal of Abnormal Psychology, 88*(6), 611–619. https://doi.org/10.1037/0021-843x.88.6.611

Krkovic, K., Clamor, A., & Lincoln, T. M. (2018). Emotion regulation as a predictor of the endocrine, autonomic, affective, and symptomatic stress response and recovery. *Psychoneuroendocrinology, 94*, 112–120. https://doi.org/10.1016/j.psyneuen.2018.04.028

Krpan, K. M., Kross, E., Berman, M. G., Deldin, P. J., Askren, M. K., & Jonides, J. (2013). An everyday activity as a treatment for depression: The benefits of expressive writing for people diagnosed with major depressive disorder. *Journal of Affective Disorders, 150*(3), 1148–1151. https://doi.org/10.1016/j.jad.2013.05.065

Kubzansky, L. D., Sparrow, D., Vokonas, P., & Kawachi, I. (2001). Is the glass half empty or half full? A prospective study of optimism and coronary heart disease in the normative aging study. *Psychosomatic Medicine, 63*(6), 910–916. https://doi.org/10.1097/00006842-200111000-00009

Lally, P., & Gardner, B. (2013). Promoting habit formation. *Health Psychology Review, 7*(sup1), S137–S158. https://doi.org/10.1080/17437199.2011.603640

Lassale, C., Batty, G. D., Baghdadli, A., Jacka, F., Sánchez-Villegas, A., Kivimäki, M., & Akbaraly, T. (2019). Healthy dietary indices and risk of depressive outcomes: A systematic review and meta-analysis of observational studies. *Molecular Psychiatry, 24*, 965–986. https://doi.org/10.1038/s41380-018-0237-8

Lin, D., Zhu, T., & Wang, Y. (2024). Emotion contagion and physiological synchrony: The more intimate relationships, the more contagion of positive emotions. *Physiology & Behavior, 275*, 114434. https://doi.org/10.1016/j.physbeh.2023.114434

Lin, F. (n.d.). *Survivors share how they are healing from their unhealthy relationships*. One Love. https://www.joinonelove.org/learn/survivors-share-how-they-are-healing-from-their-unhealthy-relationships/

Lischetzke, T. & Eid, M. (2017). The functionality of emotional clarity: A process-oriented approach to understanding the relation between emotional clarity and well-being. In: Robinson, M., Eid, M. (eds) *The happy mind: Cognitive contributions to well-being.* Springer, Cham, 371–388. https://doi.org/10.1007/978-3-319-58763-9_20

Mandriota, M. (2022, January 21). *8 foods to boost serotonin and improve mental health.* Psych Central. https://psychcentral.com/health/serotonin-foods

Marzola, P., Melzer, T., Pavesi, E., Gil-Mohapel, J., & Brocardo, P. S. (2023). Exploring the role of neuroplasticity in development, aging, and neurodegeneration. *Brain Sciences, 13*(12), 1610. https://doi.org/10.3390/brainsci13121610

Mathews, A., & MacLeod, C. (2005). Cognitive vulnerability to emotional disorders. *Annual Review of Clinical Psychology, 1*(1), 167–195. https://doi.org/10.1146/annurev.clinpsy.1.102803.143916

Meichenbaum, D. H., & Deffenbacher, J. L. (1988). Stress inoculation training. *The Counseling Psychologist, 16*(1), 69–90. https://doi.org/10.1177/0011000088161005

Meidenbauer, K. (2022, November 3). *Do physical surroundings influence our thoughts?* Psychology Today. https://www.psychologytoday.com/gb/blog/environ-mentality/202211/do-physical-surroundings-influence-our-thoughts

Molins, F., Martínez-Tomás, C., & Serrano, M. Á. (2022). Implicit negativity bias leads to greater loss aversion and learning during decision-making. *International Journal of Environmental Research and Public Health, 19*(24), 17037. https://doi.org/10.3390/ijerph192417037

Montero-Marín, J., Gaete, J., Demarzo, M., Rodero, B., Lopez, L. C. S., & García-Campayo, J. (2016). Self-Criticism: A measure of uncompassionate behaviors toward the self, based on the negative components of the self-compassion scale. *Frontiers in Psychology, 7.* https://doi.org/10.3389/fpsyg.2016.01281

Muscatell, K. A., Slavich, G. M., Monroe, S. M., & Gotlib, I. H. (2009). Stressful life events, chronic difficulties, and the symptoms of clinical depression. *The Journal of Nervous and Mental Disease, 197*(3), 154–160. https://doi.org/10.1097/nmd.0b013e318199f77b

Musich, S., Wang, S. S., Schaeffer, J. A., Kraemer, S., Wicker, E., & Yeh, C. S. (2022). The association of increasing resilience with positive health outcomes among older adults. *Geriatric Nursing, 44*, 97–104. https://doi.org/10.1016/j.gerinurse.2022.01.007

Naoumidis, A. (2019, November 22). *Thinking traps: 12 cognitive distortions that are hijacking your brain*. Mindset Health. https://www.mindsethealth.com/matter/thinking-traps-cognitive-distortions

National Heart, Lung, and Blood Institute. (2022, March 24). *What are sleep deprivation and deficiency?* https://www.nhlbi.nih.gov/health/sleep-deprivation#:~:text=Sleep%20deficiency%20can%20interfere%20with

Newsom, R., & Dimitriu, A. (2024, May 7). *Cognitive behavioral therapy for insomnia (CBT-I): An overview*. Sleep Foundation. https://www.sleepfoundation.org/insomnia/treatment/cognitive-behavioral-therapy-insomnia

Nutt, D., Wilson, S., & Paterson, L. (2008). Sleep disorders as core symptoms of depression. *Dialogues in Clinical Neuroscience, 10*(3), 329–336. https://www.ncbi.nlm.nih.gov/pmc/articles/PMC3181883/

Olatunji, B. O., Naragon-Gainey, K., & Wolitzky-Taylor, K. B. (2013). Specificity of rumination in anxiety and depression: A multimodal meta-analysis. *Clinical Psychology: Science and Practice, 20*(3), 225–257. https://doi.org/10.1111/cpsp.12037

Özdel, K., Kart, A., & Türkçapar, M. H. (2021). Cognitive behavioural therapy in treatment of bipolar disorder. *Archives of Neuropsychiatry, 58*(1) S66–S76. https://doi.org/10.29399/npa.27419

Pacheco, D. (2023, December 8). *Bedtime routines for adults*. Sleep Foundation. https://www.sleepfoundation.org/sleep-hygiene/bedtime-routine-for-adults

Pilat, D., & Krastev, S. (2021). *Negativity bias*. The Decision Lab. https://thedecisionlab.com/biases/negativity-bias

Pinilla, A., Tamayo, R. M., & Neira, J. (2020). How do induced affective states bias emotional contagion to faces? A three-dimensional model. *Frontiers in Psychology, 11*. https://doi.org/10.3389/fpsyg.2020.00097

Proulx, J., Croff, R., Oken, B., Aldwin, C. M., Fleming, C., Bergen-Cico, D., Le, T., & Noorani, M. (2018). Considerations for research and development of culturally relevant mindfulness interventions in American minority communities. *Mindfulness, 9*, 361–370. https://doi.org/10.1007/s12671-017-0785-z

Quittkat, H. L., Hartmann, A. S., Düsing, R., Buhlmann, U., & Vocks, S. (2019). Body dissatisfaction, importance of appearance, and body appreciation in men and women over the lifespan. *Frontiers in Psychiatry, 10*, 864. https://doi.org/10.3389/fpsyt.2019.00864

Renner, F., Murphy, F. C., Ji, J. L., Manly, T., & Holmes, E. A. (2019). Mental imagery as a "motivational amplifier" to promote activities. *Behaviour Research and Therapy, 114*, 51–59. https://doi.org/10.1016/j.brat.2019.02.002

Sage Neuroscience Center. (n.d.). *Breaking the cycle: Negative thought patterns.* https://sageclinic.org/blog/negative-thoughts-depression/

Sapolsky, R. M. (2000). Glucocorticoids and hippocampal atrophy in neuropsychiatric disorders. *Archives of General Psychiatry, 57*(10), 925–935. https://doi.org/10.1001/archpsyc.57.10.925

Schwartz, J. & Gladding, R. (2012). *You are not your brain: The 4-step solution for changing bad habits, ending unhealthy thinking, and taking control of your life.* Penguin Publishing Group.

Schuch, F. B., Stubbs, B., Meyer, J., Heissel, A., Zech, P., Vancampfort, D., Rosenbaum, S., Deenik, J., Firth, J., Ward, P. B., Carvalho, A. F., & Hiles, S. A. (2019). Physical activity protects from incident anxiety: A meta-analysis of prospective cohort studies. *Depression and Anxiety, 36*(9), 846–858. https://doi.org/10.1002/da.22915

Scott, A. J., Webb, T. L., Martyn-St James, M., Rowse, G., & Weich, S. (2021). Improving sleep quality leads to better mental health: A meta-analysis of randomised controlled trials. *Sleep Medicine Reviews, 60*, 101556. https://doi.org/10.1016/j.smrv.2021.101556

Segal, Z. V., Williams, M. G., & Teasdale, J. D. (2002). *Mindfulness-based cognitive therapy for depression: A new approach to preventing relapse.* Guilford Publications.

Seligman, M. E. P., Steen, T. A., Park, N., & Peterson, C. (2005). Positive psychology progress: Empirical validation of interventions. *American Psychologist, 60*(5), 410–421. https://doi.org/10.1037/0003-066x.60.5.410

Sharma, A., Madaan, V., & Petty, F. D. (2006). Exercise for mental health. *Primary Care Companion to the Journal of Clinical Psychiatry.* https://doi.org/10.4088/pcc.v08n0208a

Sissons, C. (2024, February 14). *How to boost serotonin and improve mood.* Medical News Today. https://www.medicalnewstoday.com/articles/322416

Smith, E. (2022, March 25). *What is negative thinking? How it destroys your mental health.* Healthy Place. https://www.healthyplace.com/self-help/positivity/what-is-negative-thinking-how-it-destroys-your-mental-health

Southwick, S. M., Bonanno, G. A., Masten, A. S., Panter-Brick, C., & Yehuda, R. (2014). Resilience definitions, theory, and challenges: Interdisciplinary perspectives. *European Journal of Psychotraumatology, 5*(1). https://doi.org/10.3402/ejpt.v5.25338

Sutton, J. (2020, September 24). *16 decatastrophizing tools, worksheets, and role-plays.* PositivePsychology.com. https://positivepsychology.com/decatastrophizing-worksheets/#:~:text=Magnification%20and%20filtering%20%E2%80%93%20we%20magnify

Taherkhani, Z., Kaveh, M. H., Mani, A., Ghahremani, L., & Khademi, K. (2023). The effect of positive thinking on resilience and life satisfaction of older adults: A randomized controlled trial. *Scientific Reports, 13*(1), 3478. https://doi.org/10.1038/s41598-023-30684-y

Tomasino, B., Fregona, S., Skrap, M., & Fabbro, F. (2013). Meditation-related activations are modulated by the practices needed to obtain it and by the expertise: An ALE meta-analysis study. *Frontiers in Human Neuroscience, 6,* 346 https://doi.org/10.3389/fnhum.2012.00346

Touroni, E. (2022, March 1). *Thinking traps: How to let go of negative thoughts.* The Chelsea Psychology Clinic. https://www.thechelseapsychologyclinic.com/mood-management/thinking-traps/

Tribby, A. (2022, November 8). *Cortisol and cognition: How the stress hormone affects the brain.* Aviv Clinics. https://aviv-clinics.com/blog/brain-health/how-cortisol-stress-hormone-affects-brain-health/

UCLA Health. (2018, October 17). *The link between exercise and mental health.* https://www.uclahealth.org/news/article/the-link-between-exercise-and-mental-health#:~:text=Mood%2Daltering%20benefits%20of%20exercise

Umberson, D., & Karas Montez, J. (2010). Social relationships and health: A flashpoint for health policy. *Journal of Health and Social Behavior, 51*(1_supp), S54–S66. https://doi.org/10.1177/0022146510383501

Vohs, K. D., Mead, N. L., & Goode, M. R. (2006). The psychological consequences of money. *Science, 314*(5802), 1154–1156. https://doi.org/10.1126/science.1132491

Walker, M. P. (2009). The role of sleep in cognition and emotion. *Annals of the New York Academy of Sciences, 1156*(1), 168–197. https://doi.org/10.1111/j.1749-6632.2009.04416.x

Wang, B., Zhao, Y., Lu, X., & Qin, B. (2023). Cognitive distortion based explainable depression detection and analysis technologies for the adolescent internet users on social media. *Frontiers in Public Health, 10.* https://doi.org/10.3389/fpubh.2022.1045777

WebMD Editorial Contributors. (n.d.). *What to know about 4-7-8 breathing.* WebMD. https://www.webmd.com/balance/what-to-know-4-7-8-breathing

Wenn, P., Meshoyrer, D., Barber, M., Ghaffar, A., Razka, M., Jose, S., Zeltser, R., & Makaryus, A. N. (2022). Perceived social support and its effects on treatment compliance and quality of life in cardiac patients. *Journal of Patient Experience, 9*. https://doi.org/10.1177/23743735221074170

Whalley, M. (2019, March 18). *Cognitive distortions: Unhelpful thinking habits.* Psychology Tools. https://www.psychologytools.com/articles/unhelpful-thinking-styles-cognitive-distortions-in-cbt/

Wilhelm, S., Phillips, K. A., Didie, E., Buhlmann, U., Greenberg, J. L., Fama, J. M., Keshaviah, A., & Steketee, G. (2014). Modular cognitive-behavioral therapy for body dysmorphic disorder: A randomized controlled trial. *Behavior Therapy, 45*(3), 314–327. https://doi.org/10.1016/j.beth.2013.12.007

Wright, P. (2023, November 11). *What happens in your brain when you give and practice gratitude?* Nuvance Health. https://www.nuvancehealth.org/health-tips-and-news/your-brain-when-you-give-and-practice-gratitude#:~:text=Feelings%20of%20gratitude%20can%20regulate

Wróbel, M., & Imbir, K. K. (2019). Broadening the perspective on emotional contagion and emotional mimicry: The correction hypothesis. *Perspectives on Psychological Science, 14*(3), 437-451. https://doi.org/10.1177/1745691618808523

Zanjari, N., Sharifian-sani, M., Hosseini-Chavoshi, M., Rafiey, H., & Mohammadi-Shahboulaghi, F. (2017). Successful aging as a multidimensional concept: An integrative review. *Medical Journal of the Islamic Republic of Iran, 31*(1), 686–691. https://doi.org/10.14196/mjiri.31.100

Made in United States
Troutdale, OR
03/23/2025